COMMON GROUND

Contents

At Issue: *How does the Church deal with disagreements?*

Common Ground: *The biblical account of the Jerusalem Council is our model for discussing current difficult issues.*

CHAPTER 1

Disputes in the Church

by Darlene Teague

There was great rejoicing! One of the most important and influential men in the village had made a commitment to Christ. He would no doubt persuade others in the village to become Christians. Where there had been walls to keep the Good News away, there was now an open door.

There was just one problem. One of the reasons this man was so highly respected was that he had great wealth, cattle, and numerous wives. While the wealth and cattle posed no problem in the minds of the missionaries, they had serious discussions about his multiple wives.

"No question about it. If he is going to have a positive witness for Christ, he must get rid of all his wives except for the first he married."

"Certainly, he can't be a leader. He has already violated the principle that an elder must be the husband of one wife."

"Since the Old Testament has examples of godly men with multiple wives, and since this culture is very much like the Old Testament culture, perhaps we should not question his current situation. If he sends his other wives away, they will undoubtedly end up in total poverty or be forced to become prostitutes!"

With such a range of perspectives, how could the missionaries find common ground and encourage this new believer in Christ? How would they come to an agreement when they had such a difference of opinion? How does the Church deal with disagreements like these?

Reality of Disagreements

"Difference of opinion." What images come to your mind as you reflect on those words? Various opinions and ways of seeing things are evidences that God has given each person a free will. Because of this gift that enables each of us to make choices, there are times when our options will place us on opposite sides of an issue. Sometimes we will find that both (or all) opinions on an issue are valid and within the bounds of God's grace. However, there are times when we must distinguish between the areas of freedom and the areas that cannot be compromised. Many Christians reflect the attitude of the familiar saying, "In essentials, unity; in non-essentials, liberty; in all things, charity." The task before us is to determine how to recognize the essential or necessary things, how to offer freedom to each other in those nonessential areas, and how to resolve conflict about the necessary things.

Among the earliest followers of Christ, we find both unity and diversity. Since the first Christians were Jewish, the early believers took for granted that followers of Christ would also practice Jewish customs and laws. While the faith was still "in Jerusalem, and . . . Judea" (Acts 1:8), that assumption seemed accurate. However, once people accepted the message of Christ in "Samaria, and to the ends of the earth," the Gentile converts started to ask why they should hold to Jewish law. The most crucial of the questions concerned circumcision. Since circumcision was the sign of being part of God's chosen people, those of Jewish background insisted that men who converted to Christ from outside the Jewish faith had to be circumcised. Those converts argued they had been made God's children through faith in Christ Jesus and did not need to be circumcised. Obviously, this difference of perspective and opinion became a point of conflict and tension among the believers.

Just as the early Christian church had issues resulting in friction, throughout history there have been those areas that were open for diversity and areas that could not be compromised. What are some of today's issues that result in disagreements, misunderstandings, and conflict? Some of the areas we might quickly identify have to do with the church building and facilities. How should we decorate the building? Can outside groups use our church facilities? Should a particular function be held in the sanctuary or in the fellowship hall?

Another category has to do with programming in the church. Should we operate a daycare center or Christian school? What about nonchurch programs like scouting, mothers' groups, or aerobic exercise classes? What worship services must be part of our regular schedule?

A third category addresses personal practices of members. Can a person be a part of our church and still go to movies, drink socially, or not be baptized? What if someone wants to become a member of our church yet they hold to different doctrinal distinctives? How much difference in how we understand God can we tolerate?

Any of these categories can result in tensions or even divisions in a church. How can we address issues in such a way that we remain true to biblical principles while preserving the spirit of unity among the Body? One of the techniques we must use is to identify the common ground on which we stand. For all the details that can bring division, there is a core of issues where we find total agreement. Whether we are one denomination or another, whether we are from one culture or another, whether we have one passion of ministry or another, we are intricately bound together by the Holy Spirit.

Even as we celebrate our unity through the Holy Spirit, we struggle to resolve various issues that threaten to divide us. We are Christians, but we are also members of a particular congregation or denomination. We must make a

conscious effort to identify those things within our traditions that cannot be compromised before we can enter into productive dialogue regarding other issues. There are
some practices that are contrary to God's Word and a
range of acceptable practices in other areas. For example,
all Christians agree that murder is sin and cannot be condoned if one is truly a Christian. However, because there
are some Christians who are pacifists and others who are
career military personnel, we have degrees of understanding about if and when one human being can kill another.

The Biblical Model

The Jerusalem Council, recorded in Acts 15, provides
a standard for handling disagreements in the Church.

Some of the Christians from Judea traveled to Antioch
with a surprising message. According to them, unless a
person was circumcised, he could not be a Christian.
News of their teaching reached Paul and Barnabas, who
were also in Antioch. Paul and Barnabas disagreed with
these messengers. The Bible says they engaged in "sharp
dispute and debate" (v. 2). Both parties believed their
opinions represented the truth. However, this was an issue
where both could not be correct. Either circumcision was
necessary for salvation, or it was not.

In order to come to an "official" position, the church
sent Paul and Barnabas, along with some other believers, to
meet with the church leaders in Jerusalem. As they traveled
from Antioch to Jerusalem, Paul and Barnabas told the believers along the way how the Gentiles had come to Christ.
They gave the same report to the officials in Jerusalem.

Not all were ready to offer an unqualified welcome to
the Gentile believers. A group of Christians, who had been
Pharisees in the Jewish faith, declared that Gentile believers had to be circumcised and follow the Mosaic law before they could truly be Christians.

The apostles and elders met to discuss this question

of what the Gentiles had to do or not do to become part of the Christian church. According to Acts 15:7, it took much discussion for them to come to a consensus of opinion. Somewhere in the process, Peter stood and spoke in defense of those who came to Christ through faith. He told how God made no distinction between the Jew and the Gentile; each is saved through the grace of Jesus Christ. Following Peter's speech, Paul and Barnabas told of all God had been doing among the Gentiles. The whole assembly listened carefully to their accounts.

James summarized the reports and offered scriptural support to the events Peter and the others had observed. James expressed his opinion that they ought not make it difficult for the Gentiles to be accepted into the family of faith. He listed the requirements that were important for the new believers and the Christian faith. James directed that all those who choose to follow Christ should "abstain from food polluted by idols, from sexual immorality, from the meat of strangled animals and from blood" (v. 20). Circumcision was notably absent from his list, especially since this was the issue that had prompted the meeting. He instead focused on those things that could cause a person to fall away from following Christ. He also noted that in those places housing a synagogue, Gentiles had long had the opportunity to accept the Jewish faith, but becoming Jewish first was not necessary.

The entire assembly agreed with James and wrote a letter containing the requirements for Christians. They selected two from the council, Judas and Silas, to accompany Paul and Barnabas to deliver the letter in Antioch. When the people received the letter, they were glad and encouraged by it.

Applying the Biblical Model in Today's Setting

While there is great value in learning the story in Acts 15, there is also usefulness in discovering how we can apply the biblical principles to situations we face today. How can the principles that we find in Acts 15 direct us as we discuss difficult issues in the Church?

Principle One: Seek guidance of the Holy Spirit.

First and foremost, we must follow the example of the Early Church by looking to the Holy Spirit to guide us. We will not solve difficult—or even easy—issues unless He helps us. We want to have all our efforts guided by His light, rather than looking only to our own wisdom and knowledge. It is difficult enough to discern what the basis of a difference is without our egos affecting how we look at it. The Holy Spirit can prompt people to say the very things we all need to hear in order to draw biblically sound conclusions.

Principle Two: Everyone's opinion should be heard, though we may not agree with every opinion.

If you have ever participated in a "brainstorming session," you have likely heard the leader say something like, "There are no bad or wrong ideas. Every suggestion is worth hearing." When we are seriously trying to find the common ground in the church, we must welcome and listen to all sincere opinions. Each person's thoughts are important to the process. Allowing a person to express a personal opinion or particular viewpoint validates that person. Let me explain. By listening to an opinion without voicing an immediate judgment on it, we show respect for another person. We are saying in effect, "What you *think* is important because *you* are important." When we immediately reject an idea or thought, we are saying, "You and your ideas are not valid here."

In fact, when we are hearing various views on an issue, there will be ideas we don't accept. The most obvious value in listening to all first before making conclusions is simply this: we may be wrong. We may have the best intentions, but we may need to adjust our thinking. We are acting in loving humility when we listen to every person's idea. We are obedient to the Holy Spirit when we accept correction.

Principle Three: Focus on the issue rather than the personalities behind the differing opinions.

We must train ourselves to ask the Holy Spirit to keep our focus on the issue and not on the person who is offering an opinion. If we look at the person, we may find reasons to discredit his or her thoughts when, in fact, he or she offers a valid (and sometimes crucial) view of the issue.

Let's face it. Some people just rub us the wrong way. No matter what they say, they say it in such a way that we take a defensive stance. It may be their tone; perhaps it is the way they phrase their remarks. It may be they have offended us in the past, or they have the reputation of being odd. The bottom line is that whenever they start to say anything, we tune them out.

When we focus on the person, we are looking in the wrong direction. When someone we don't want to hear begins to speak, we need to ask the Holy Spirit to open our ears to hear what He may be trying to say through that person. We need to ask the Holy Spirit to help us keep our focus on the issue.

Principle Four: Difficult issues and decisions require hard work.

We may as well say it openly. There are no easy answers. We wish there were. We try to bring an issue (or series of issues) down to a simple statement. The truth is that some of the questions of life and faith do not have easy answers. For those of us who would like a system that is, in every detail of life, absolutely "black and white," we may become frustrated. However, the fact there are often equally correct, yet different answers shows us a glimpse of the grace of God. For example, there are some churches that divide teaching groups into male and female. There are men teachers for the male groups and women teachers for the female groups. In their setting, they prefer to not have "mixed gender" classes. Another church (perhaps even in the same community) has classes grouped by age or interest, regardless of gender. They believe it is important for men and women to learn from each other because they value having the opposite gender's perspective on life. Is one more biblical or "right" than the other? No. Each has rational reasons and biblical support for their choice. God's grace allows room for both interpretations.

Finding our common ground is hard work. Just look again at the folks in Jerusalem. There were some very strong and long-standing traditions that were being challenged. Some there couldn't imagine a person could be an uncircumcised Christian.

Principle Five: Authority of the Bible and our leaders need to be respected.

At some point in the process, a leader or voice of authority must be heard. In Acts 15, James served as the authority in the council. When he spoke, the rest of the participants listened—and agreed—to his summary.

Since we hold that the Word of God is the final authority in our faith and practice, we must certainly draw first from its teaching. We also utilize three other means of discerning the truth. Reason (does this make sense?), tradition (how has the question been answered in the past?), and experience (what impact of the decision can we see or have we seen?) aid us in making a wise decision.

Principle Six: Draw conclusions that promote unity while respecting differences.

Once we have sought the guidance of the Holy Spirit, listened to everyone who wanted to speak to the issue, weighed the various options in light of the Bible, reason, tradition, and experience, then we are ready to draw our conclusions. As we identify the nonnegotiable issues and decide the best course of action, we also make every effort to respect the differences that are not settled. In other words, our decision to find unity in one area will not be at the expense of unity in another area.

The good news is that with prayerful hard work, we can find the common ground. Once we identify the truly vital issues and stand together on them, then we can allow one another the freedom to have different opinions in nonessential areas.

Background Scripture: Mark 10:7-8; Acts 1:8; 15:1-33; 1 Corinthians 7:17-24

About the Author: Darlene Teague is a curriculum editor at the International Headquarters of The Wesleyan Church in Indianapolis.

At Issue: *What does it mean to be created in God's image? How are we creators? How are we tempted to pervert our creative nature?*

Common Ground: *We believe humans are created in God's image, but with different creative powers. Only God created from nothing, but we continue to create the world in which we live in many ways.*

CHAPTER 2

Created in God's Image
by Joseph Coleson

Hardly a verse in all the Bible is more sublime or more important than Genesis 1:27. Here is my translation (similar to most translations you have read), "So God created the *'adam* [the human race] in His image; in the image of God He created it [the human race]; male and female He created them."

Human beings are created in God's image. God created *all* humans in God's own image. Whatever else Christians and Jews say about God, about people, and about theology—and we say a lot!—we agree that God created all humans in God's image.

What Does It Mean to Be Created in God's Image?

What does it mean that we are created *imago Dei* (ih-MAH-go DAY-ee), "in the image of God"? What does it mean for our attitudes, our behavior, and our destiny? Did the Fall destroy all that God originally intended for it to mean? These, and many other serious, yet hopeful, questions arise out of this extraordinary verse.

We should note, first, that creation in God's image does *not* mean we are divine. God is transcendent and infinite; we are not. The Judeo-Christian faith affirms that God is entirely good, all-knowing, and all-powerful, and is not limited by the boundaries of time or space, since time and space, too, are God's creations. Humanity's original goodness was a created goodness, while God's goodness is self-originating and transcendent (above or beyond creation). The other attributes—all-knowing, all-powerful, and not limited by time or space—are God's because God is transcendent. Contrary to several popular faith systems, humans never were, are not now, and never will be like God in these respects. God alone is transcendent and infinite. We are divinely created, but we are not divine.

So what *are* we? As the species of this earth whose life begins in the breath/spirit of God (Genesis 2:7), what is "human being"? What does it mean to be created in the image of God? It means, at least, that we embody personality, spirit, will, intellect, wisdom, emotion, self-consciousness, humor, language, community, and creativity. Let us focus for now on creativity, partly because creativity usually draws on several other of these characteristics for its full expression, partly because in the exercise of creativity we often are tempted to overvalue ourselves and to undervalue God, our created brothers and sisters, and the rest of God's creation.

How Are Humans Creators?

God created ex nihilo (a Latin phrase meaning "out of nothing"). Obviously, humans cannot create ex nihilo. If that were all we could say, it would end the discussion. However, there is more.

First, God's creation did not end with one, or even with several, acts ex nihilo. Accounts and/or celebrations of God's creative acts on this earth are scattered through several sections of the Bible, beginning, of course, with Genesis 1—2. Each individually, and all of them together, accent God's joy and satisfaction in the creative *process,* as well as in the creative *outcome.* God creates, in part, for the joy of the making; but also, in part, for the beauty of, for the usefulness of, and for God's satisfaction in the finished creation. When God creates using material and energy God has previously brought into being, God takes joy in making something out of something. When we create using materials and energy God has previously brought into being, we show our creation in God's image by taking joy in making something out of something.

We do continually create and re-create the world in which we live in many ways, some for good and some for ill. In doing so, we exercise our creation mandate of Genesis 1:28. God did not rescind this mandate even in the face of the certainty that we would misuse it and betray the trust vested in it after our first parents declared their independence from God, in the event that we call, in theological terms, the Fall.

When we use the term *creative* of a human, we often think of original compositions in music; of original paintings, photos, sculptures, and such in the visual arts; of original poetry, novels, essays, and other forms in the literary arts. Still, human creativity is as broad and as deep as human activity. Cooks create new dishes; athletes create new moves and strategies, even whole new games and sports. Academics create new descriptions, new explanations, whole new disciplines. Engineers create new structures and new systems. Every building, from a backyard shed to a facility covering 40 acres of ground under one roof, is an expression of human creativity. Entrepreneurs create new products and new markets. Even lovers create ways to say "I love you" that, if not exactly new, at least are new to those two people enjoying them for the first time.

Imagine a lens that could provide a view that was at the same time wide-angle and telescopic. Imagine further that this lens could provide a rapid time-lapse progression of images through the several thousand years of Middle Eastern history, or through the several hundred years since the European arrival in the Americas. Anyone privileged to look through such a lens could not doubt that humans exercise enormous creative impact on the earth's environmental systems. In those regions, and in others, we literally have changed the face of the earth. Some of this impact is destructive, some of it is constructive, but all of it is "creative" in the sense that it is the result of human beings working to alter conditions as we have found them.

Please, God, I'd Rather Do It Myself!

God's creative activity is always good because God is good and God is wise. Humans create because we are created in the image of God. Our creative activity is not always for good, however, because we decided early on to gain for ourselves the knowledge of evil.

We must stress again that God did issue to the human race the mandate to exercise stewardship over this earth (Genesis 1:28). God gave this mandate in the form of a command—actually, a series of five imperative verbs; "[you all, female and male] be fruitful"; "[you all, male and female] multiply"; "[you all, female and male] fill the earth"; "[you all, male and female] subdue it [the earth]"; "[you all, female and male] exercise stewardship dominion over [the other creatures]."

God commissioned the human race to tend, care for, keep, watch, and protect the rest of God's creation on this earth. God placed the first 'adam (human) in the garden to "serve it and to keep it" (2:15). God could not more clearly and firmly have *excluded* exploitation of all the earthly creation than by using these two verbs.

Yet, the first pair turned from God, preferring to believe the lie that they would be "as God" (3:5). Ever since, the human race too often has discharged God's mandate to exercise dominion over the earth in irresponsible and destructive ways, abandoning stewardship to embrace exploitation. Often, this has been because of ignorance or inattention, as when poor tillage practices have turned vast areas of prime agricultural land into dustbowls and deserts. Sometimes, exploitation rises from the belief that a given resource is so abundant it could not possibly be depleted. Examples in the United States are the bison that almost vanished and the passenger pigeon that did—both through overhunting.

Sometimes we know but do not care, preferring to exalt greed and profit over responsible stewardship of the earth. This is currently the case with several of the great fisheries of the seas and several of the remaining expanses of timber in the Americas and in Southeast Asia.

Even more tragic (so far in human history, at least) has been our will to dominate each other. Humans often neglect the creative attention needed "to serve and to keep" the earth, and concentrate our creativity, instead, on finding ways to dominate and exploit fellow humans, our brothers and sisters in creation.

The earth and its creatures, including us, suffer much when we refuse or are afraid to use our powers of observation and reasoning in creative, imaginative, and constructive ways. Sadly, we wreak much havoc from the opposite direction, also, using our creative powers in many marvelous and ingenious ways to advance our own short-term interests, not knowing or not caring about the devastation our God-given intelligence and creativity bring about when we refuse to use them reverently and wisely.

Surely, Christians do not have a problem with this, do we? We know we are responsible to God for our stewardship of the earth, its creatures, and its resources, and for our treatment of each other. How could we be guilty of perverting our creativity?

We must begin with the observation, a truism by now, that we live in a post-Christian age. That means, basically, that our culture no longer operates in conscious regard for God and God's ways. We do our own thing, guided only by pragmatism as our philosophical lodestar: "Does it work? Then do it."

This means the Church is called to be countercultural,

to confront the culture with its shortcomings by living according to a different value system, by "marching to a different drummer." But so far, in the post-Christian age, the Church has had difficulty understanding this, to say nothing of practicing it.

Individual Christians often go days, years, and entire careers, never asking themselves seriously, "What does it mean for me to be a Christian outside my house of worship?" We pursue goals that come naturally in our culture, by methods natural to our culture, never asking whether God approves, whether these goals and methods bring glory to God, or whether they are bringing other people to consider God and God's offer of grace.

It is no wonder individual Christians so seldom bring their lives, including their creativity, radically under the lordship of God. The evangelical North American church has been taken willing captive to secular human methods of leadership and evaluation, methods that work against the vision of every person as infinitely loved and valued by the God who created him or her. We have adopted, almost without exception, the corporate CEO, hierarchical, top-down leadership style in our local churches and in our denominations. We have adopted corporate accounting systems for evaluating success, reckoning success by the totals of bodies and dollars, while neglecting or minimizing persons, personal relationships, and the value God places on each and every individual human being.

The Church as a whole, both individually and collectively, has erred on the side of planning and acting as though humanly framed goals pursued by means of human methodologies are adequate to accomplish God's purposes. Individual Christians have used their creativity to pursue their own goals, without regard to the God who gave it. As individuals and as the Church collectively, too often we have said, "Please, God, I'd rather do it myself!"

The Other Extreme: "Worm Theology"

The other extreme exists. Not nearly so many individuals fall into it, and no organizations, so far as can be determined. Yet, when embraced, it is equally fatal to godly use of our God-given creative powers. "Worm theology" takes its name from the line in Isaac Watts's hymn, "Would He devote that sacred head for such a worm as I?"

As a statement of our hopeless condition before God's grace reached us, that line has merit. As a statement of our intrinsic value to God that caused God to reach out in grace, despite the staggering cost to God, it is utterly misleading and inadequate. As a guide to behavior for the redeemed son or daughter of the King of the universe, it would be laughable were it not so tragic in its consequences. We are not worms. God's redeeming grace calls us to act like men and women in training to rule kingdoms, spheres, and galaxies—for that is who we are.

Worm theology comes in two varieties, the individual and the group. The individual says, "I'm just a worm. I'm inadequate. Nothing I could do could have any effect. It wouldn't be valuable or important, and, besides, it probably wouldn't work, anyway."

The group says, "All humans are worms. All our actions are hopelessly sin-infected. All we can do is adopt an ascetic life, steep ourselves in penitence, prayer, and contemplation, and hope that God soon will bring the end." Like the individual worm, the group (the can of worms?) renounces God's gift of creativity. Like the third servant in Jesus' famous parable (Matthew 25:14-30), in worm theology both the individual and the group bury in the ground the talents they have received, and hope God will not notice because of the fervency of their prayers and their devotion.

So, Where Is the Common Ground?

While we have been hard both on "gung-ho, let's go"

and on "worm" theology as we have considered the two positions in isolation, it is easy to see that, in partnership, these two can be powerful motivating forces. It is not "either" initiative "or" contemplation. It is *both* initiative *and* contemplation. We need both the doers and the prayers. We need initiative and creativity of the type that says, "In Christ, I/we can do this." We need also the realism about sin and human weakness that says, "Without Christ, I/we cannot even begin to do this."

We are called to use our creative powers to find ways to promote human worth in our dehumanizing culture, worth based on the assurance that each individual is a precious creation in God's image. We must use our creativity to learn to live in ways that call our culture to account for its oppressive greed and callous disregard for those with no access to power. We are called to be creative in founding and multiplying communities, fellowships, and systems that validate people and meet their needs—physical, economic, social, and spiritual. We are called to live simply with taste and creativity—to exercise good stewardship upon the earth, to be sure, but more importantly to have time, money, and self to give to and for the poor and the unreached. We are called to live "Christianly" in a post-Christian age!

Background Scripture: Genesis 1—2; 3:5; Matthew 25:14-30

About the Author: Dr. Coleson, an ordained elder in The Wesleyan Church, is professor of Hebrew Scriptures at Nazarene Theological Seminary, Kansas City.

At Issue: How are Christians responsible for relationships within the Church? Are Christians responsible for the world outside the Church?

Common Ground: God created us for relationship with Him and responsibility for others.

CHAPTER 3

Created for a Purpose

by Joseph Coleson

The people who keep track of such things tell us that for much of history the human population of the world hovered around 200 million. It took until about 1830 to reach the first billion in population. Then sometime in October 1999 the earth's human population passed 6 billion. Older citizens remember a time when the earth supported half as many people as are alive today. To illustrate in another way, when the 13 colonies won their independence from Great Britain, their population was about 4 million. Today, the population of the United States exceeds 260 million, more than 65 times as many persons.

How can one person imagine himself or herself to be significant when more than 6 billion other people live on earth, when the net gain in world population every day is more than 100,000 persons? With so many of us in existence, can any one of us have real meaning to God, to ourselves, or to anyone?

We Are Here to Connect

The "great" or "ultimate" questions sometimes are framed: "Who are we?" "Where did we come from?" "Why are we here?" In the last chapter, in exploring human creativity as an aspect of the image of God in which we are created, we dealt in part with the first two questions. In asserting as a kind of thesis statement that we are created for relationship and responsibility to God and to our human brothers and sisters, we now deal, in part, with the third question.

One of the influential Protestant catechisms answers the third question as follows: "The chief end of [humans] is to glorify God and enjoy Him forever." The words *glorify* and *enjoy* assume both relationship and responsibility.

Genesis 3:8 is a glimpse, a vignette, of God's habit of, and God's joy in, coming daily to commune with the two humans in the garden in the "cool of the day." "Cool" is, literally, the "breath," "wind," or "breeze" of the day. Near large bodies of water, for example, it is the time in the afternoon when the sea breeze rises in the summertime to temper the overpowering heat of the day. At this most delightful time of day, God delighted in coming to walk and talk with the man and the woman. God created them for relationship with Him and with each other; in the garden their relationship was a delight to God and to them. Every day, God connected with the man and the woman, and they with God.

The man and woman, by their disobedience and rebellion, broke the connection. In breaking their fellowship with God, they found it impossible to maintain their fellowship with each other. Ever since, we humans have felt our estrangement from God and have attempted to replace our lost intimate communion with each other. Most often, we err at one or the other of two extremes. On the one hand, we rush into premature and unwise intimacy, sabotaging the very thing we so desperately long for. Or, on the other hand, we attempt with all our might to dominate each other in a lunatic effort to compel those very qualities and attitudes that cannot be compelled: admiration, esteem, respect, faithfulness, love. We seem trapped in a maze without an exit. Is there a way out? Can the rupture be repaired? Will the connection ever be restored?

R = 2R

Mathematically, of course, the above equation is impossible, if "R" possesses the same nonzero value on both sides of the equation, as it must for mathematical language to make sense. As we think about the restoration of the Genesis 3:8 relationship, we are dealing here with something equally impossible in merely human terms. Once the divine-human and human-human relationships were ruptured, no merely human initiative could restore or repair them. Only God could do that. To restore the broken relationships, God would have to want to do so. The wonder is that God did want to, and God did it.

Redemption equals restored relationship (R = 2R). Our Reformation heritage conditions us to think of redemption mainly in forensic (or legal) terms. Christ's redemptive work on the Cross satisfied God's legal conditions for our forgiveness. This is true, but it by no means exhausts the whole concept of redemption and forgiveness.

Forgiveness is a door, but even guests do not go into a home and stand just inside the door for their whole visit. The redeemed are much more than guests; we are the sons and daughters of the King, the sisters and brothers of the Crown Prince.

Redemption restores relationship. In Christ, we again have relationship with God and continue, then, to build relationship with God. In Christ, we again have relationship with our fellow human beings and continue, then, to build and improve relationships with them.

The Church Is God's Portrait of Community

Paul's extended metaphor in 1 Corinthians 12:12-27 is a beautiful and vivid picture of this intimacy and interdependency of community as God intends it in the fellowship of the redeemed. In picturing the Church as a human body, Paul emphasized that every Christian is important. Yes, a body can continue to live without some of its members, but it never can be complete without them, never perfect as God intended. Every member is essential.

Every member also depends on many other members.

In a real sense, every member of the Body of Christ depends on every other member. We hold each other up in prayer, even if not by name. We bear each other's burdens, even when we don't know we are. We inspire each other to faithfulness just by our own everyday faithfulness. We really do need each other.

Members of both the human body and the Church Paul depicts by his use of the body metaphor are not only essential and functionally interdependent but also beautiful works of God's skillful, caring, intimate, and loving creation. The body and the Church are beautiful as their members are beautiful. The beauty of the image of God is reflected *in* each and *to* each.

That we are and must be continuously in relationship with God is self-evident. So are we, and so must we be, in unbroken relationship with our brothers and sisters in the Body of Christ. Redemption equals restored relationship, in community with each other, as well as with God.

Since we are finite and localized in our humanity, this happens concretely in the local fellowship of believers, the local church or congregation. There is no room for mere abstraction in the Christian faith. We exercise relationship only as we relate directly and concretely with other people. We worship God together and grow together in love for God and for each other. You meet a real need; someone meets your real need. I say "God bless you" to a real person; she says "God bless you too" to me. Relationship happens person-to-person. At its best, relationship happens face-to-face.

We All Are 'Adam

Besides the name of the first man, 'Adam is also God's name for the human race (Genesis 1:26-28; 2:18-24; 5:1-2; etc.). As members of the human race, we are mutually members one of another. We share innumerable mutual, vital interests by virtue of being 'adam, human, created in the image of and carrying the breath of God. As C. S. Lewis put it, our neighbor (any human) quite possibly is the most sacred object ever presented to our senses, because we all are created *imago Dei,* in the image of God.

As humans, we share common vital interests on many fronts. What is good for any one of us will be, in normal circumstances, good for all of us. What is bad for any one of us will be bad for all of us. We all need air, water, food, clothing, shelter, useful work, intimate relationships. By reason of our common humanity, the already-redeemed and the not-yet-redeemed are bound together in myriad and diverse ways. Because—and solely because—we are human, our true interests converge many times more often than they diverge. Every human being is our brother or our sister in creation.

The Fall marred, but did not destroy, the image of God in *'adam* [human]. The Fall disrupted the original relationships between God and *'adam,* and between *'adam* and *'adam.* Redemption restored the relationship between God and *'adam,* and between *'adam* and *'adam.* That was God's purpose before the foundation of the world; it is God's purpose in making redemption available to all. God's redemptive intention is second only to our kinship in creation as a reason for regarding ourselves brother or sister to every *'adam,* whether they be "Jews or Greeks, slave or free" (1 Corinthians 12:13).

So *How* Do We Connect?

Thus far, few thinking Christians will disagree on any point vital to the issues we are discussing. However, when it comes to how we are to relate to each other, whether within the Church or to those who do not share the Christian faith, Christians are all over the map, literally and figuratively.

The pressures on the Body of Believers are, in some ways, greater now than at any other time since Constantine embraced the faith. We live in a culture that is post-

Christian in all its leading indicators, in virtually every arena where influential people shape public opinion. While most European, United States, and Canadian Christians lead "traditional" western Christian lives, western culture becomes more and more post-Christian, more and more hostile to Christians and to Christian values.

At the same time, most western nations are already multiethnic and multicultural in their citizenry. Several cities in Europe and in North America have speakers of over 100 languages in their populations. Every hue of faith and nonfaith is represented among the religious beliefs and practices of most western nations' populations.

How should traditional western Christians respond to the conversion of our own nations and communities to a post-Christian culture and to the multiculturalism that characterizes every urban area and, increasingly, even many rural areas? Can we address these issues in integrity and faithfulness to God, while making known the good news of God's redemptive work in Christ to those who are different from us in faith, in ethnicity, and/or in culture?

The "Least Is Best" Approach

One answer has been to reduce our understanding of the faith to the lowest common denominator. This approach contains an element of truth. We should recognize that much more unites us within the Christian faith than ever could divide us. We should acknowledge the unity of the faith, as well as the diversity of emphasis and practice across the spectrum of Christianity.

Nevertheless, an all-consuming emphasis on organic unity and/or unity of practice-in-detail sacrifices too much. Diversity of emphases in formulations of faith, in worship practice, in the ministry of the Body of Christ around the world, are all vital to meeting the needs of the Church in the diversity of places where it exists and to the evangelization of the not-yet-redeemed.

A further danger of this approach is that it too easily leads to loss of anything that is distinctively Christian. It leads to the muting of our witness to the Redeemer, in our desire to avoid offending those who need to hear that witness. Instead of expending our energies in creative and loving service and witness, we dissipate them in "not offending."

The Fortress Mentality

The opposite approach has been to erect fortresses with strong, high walls and put up large signs that say, "Keep out, unless you are just like us." In our efforts to grow the church quickly, we succumb to the allure of the homogeneity principle, which says the church grows fastest when it welcomes people just like the ones already there. Divisions of social and economic status, ethnic, and/or language identity arise and become entrenched. Local congregations become a series of fortresses, keeping out not only "the world" but all Christians who don't look, act, or think just like them.

Just as tragically, we sometimes build fortresses on narrow points of doctrine, "purifying" the church by reducing it in size to the "faithful few." We say, "If you don't agree with us *exactly* on *every* point of doctrine, you cannot be part of us, and probably you are a heretic. We'll pray for your soul, but don't come around here trying to contaminate us." Orthodoxy (right teaching) is everything; orthopraxy (right doing)—as in demonstrating Christ's love and confidence—is neglected.

Perhaps worst of all is the fortress mentality that lumps all non-Christians and all "not like us" Christians together and brands them as "devils," or as "of the devil." Charity (love) toward outsiders becomes an evil. The suffering of outsiders is greeted with joy as the just wrath of God. The end is near, and only "we" will be spared; God's love extends only to us.

What, Then?

So what is the right approach? How do we have relationship with responsibility toward God and toward our fellow humans, both Christian and non-Christian? We begin by relating with integrity and faithfulness to God. The Christian faith is unique precisely because it is God's revelation. It was God's initiative to reestablish relationship when we were the ones who broke relationship. Christians have less than nothing to offer anyone else if we do not continue in faithful relationship to the God who has called us.

In the love, wisdom, and confidence of that relationship with God, Christians then can approach non-Christians (and other suspicious or hostile Christians too) with love, justice, mercy, kindness, openness, generosity, service, and confidence. In Christ, gender, ethnic, language, social, economic, or any other differences never can be a basis for exclusion. Rather, they become catalysts for reflection on and rejoicing in the amazing breadth and depth of God's love, grace, and mercy extended to all, to every 'adam.

The difference between the already-redeemed and the not-yet-redeemed is the difference between the already-rescued-from-spiritual-death and the not-yet-rescued-from-spiritual-death. The Christian is already alive in Christ. The not-yet-Christian is, nevertheless, still human by reason of creation in God's image, still a candidate for life in Christ.

Christians, therefore, are free to act as members of the body *politic*, as well as to act as members of the body *ecclesial*, to use classical, formal terms. We are members of the Church, the Body of Christ, but we also are members of the human race. We may act in concert with our fellow humans. We may associate with them in moral, ethical, just pursuits. Real problems beset our culture, our nations, our communities. Christians can and should participate in the marketplace, modeling godliness in every public and private arena.

More importantly, from the perspective of eternity, such participation is a witness to God's redemptive purpose for all (and each) 'adam. Responsible interaction with our brothers and sisters in creation eventually earns the right to speak of God's passionate desire that they become also our brothers and sisters in redemption. Redemption equals restored relationship.

Background Scripture: Genesis 1:26-28; 2:18-24; 3:8; 5:1-2; 1 Corinthians 12:12-27

About the Author: Dr. Coleson, an ordained elder in The Wesleyan Church, is professor of Hebrew Scriptures at Nazarene Theological Seminary, Kansas City.

At Issue: Is it wrong for Christians to work hard and provide material comforts, or should we depend entirely on God to supply our needs? What is the economic impact of our lifestyles?

Common Ground: God is the One who provides all we need, have, and enjoy, and we are to be responsible managers of all He provides.

CHAPTER 4

Standard of Living
by Mark A. Holmes

The unofficial state bird of Wisconsin is the mosquito. Now I know you will point out that mosquitoes are insects. However, you have not experienced the winged creatures that thrive around my house. They are everywhere, gathering in massive clouds resembling Hitchcock's *The Birds* in ferocity. Their proboscises feel like a bird's beak. We are talking California condor here! Their presence and attack has left me wondering why God created them in the first place and why Noah didn't swat the two when he had the chance. I know they have a purpose within creation, but could not God have filled their niche with a less bloodthirsty creature?

This question opens a broader inquiry—why the creation at all, and how do we relate to it? In response, Christians have embraced a number of common agreements:

1. There exists a personal living God (John 1:1).
2. This personal, living God is the creator of everything that is not God (John 1:3).
3. The purpose of this creation is to beget and sustain life for fellowship with God (Genesis 2:8-9).
4. God has set humanity at a unique position, to interact with God, creation, and itself (Genesis 1:28-30).

It almost seems ridiculous to list the existence of God as a common ground of agreement among Christians. Such a reality is as necessary for the Christian faith as air is for life. But the reality of God's existence calls for us to recognize the need of relating to Him. God is not a part of creation, but is still found within it. God is not the result of creation, but its very source.

This brings us to our second point of agreement, God created all that exists that is not itself God. This reality is expressed to us in the Gospel of John (as cited above), and illustrated by the first two chapters of Genesis. The common ground among Christians is our willingness to ascribe to God the credit for causing our present creation.

Creation has a specific purpose. It is the means by which God can relate to something other than himself. If point 2 above is correct, then prior to creation there existed only God fellowshipping with himself within the Trinity. Christians believe that when God created the heavens and the earth, the basic building material used—matter—was not in existence. God created all there is from nothing, providing a means for Him to relate to something other than himself.

At the apex of creation, God uniquely made humanity with some attributes different from all of creation. Genesis explains this by stating that God created us in His image (Genesis 1:26), God breathed into humanity a special life force we refer to as our soul (2:7), and God placed us within creation with the task of overseeing and populating the world (1:28-29). This unique position places humanity in an awkward situation. We are part of creation and commanded to control it, but we are not to get so caught up with it that we neglect our primary responsibility to fellowship with God. The Creation has become accepted as a type of rental unit we inhabit until our eternal mansions are completed in heaven (John 14:3). Our challenge now is to live within this creation without allowing its negative influence to take precedence over God. We cannot separate ourselves from the world, as we are dependant upon it for our very existence. Still, Jesus commissioned us to go into the midst of the world as His ambassadors without becoming a part of it (17:13-21).

Here then is our present dilemma: Humanity, created in God's image, enlivened by His breath for fellowship with Him, is also made of the substance of creation, influenced and sustained by its very elements, responsible for its control, care, and population. Yet, we must refuse its rule in favor of a relationship with God. What are we to do? How do we settle this universal dilemma of relationship?

One major place where this tension is felt is in the area of life's provisions. We can succeed in maintaining a separation between creation and ourselves in any other area and still survive, except for this. Created from the elements of this world, we are totally dependent upon our interaction with it in order to obtain the essentials for life. The tension is found in the understanding that no matter how dependent we might be upon something, that dependence cannot replace our primary relationship with God. Therefore, where do we draw the line between dependency and self-sufficiency? What is God's responsibility and what is humanity's?

Jesus discusses this tension in His Sermon on the Mount (Matthew 5—7). Gathered around Him that day, eavesdropping, was the familiar, large, desperate crowd of people who followed Him. Contained within the truths Jesus was sharing with His disciples was a lesson on balancing our dependence upon creation for earthly existence while also developing our future eternal existence. His disciples needed to hear these words, because they would soon be commissioned as itinerant preachers without home or income. The crowd that was listening was quite likely unemployed or in some kind of great need. Living in a society that afforded little of the securities we have today, these people were challenged by physical survival every day. To the disciples and crowd, Jesus said:

Therefore I tell you, do not worry about your life,

what you will eat or drink; or about your body, what you will wear. Is not life more important than food, and the body more important than clothes? . . . So do not worry, saying, "What shall we eat?" or "What shall we drink?" or "What shall we wear?" For the pagans run after all these things, and your heavenly Father knows that you need them. But seek first his kingdom and his righteousness, and all these things will be given to you as well *(Matthew 6:25, 31-33)*.

Several applications can be derived from this regarding our dilemma. In general, our physical existence is not to be a primary concern. This is apparent with Jesus' continued command to not allow anxiety over our existence to control us. Yet, considering the gravity of the issue, it is hard to not feel the very concern prohibited. In place of anxiety we are to embrace several alternate realities.

Although the physical may be the most immediate, it is not the primary need. We often determine priorities by chronology. Those issues that will challenge us first are what we care for most. If we view our spiritual existence as something that will take place years from now upon our physical death, then it seems quite natural to apply our energies toward what will take place within the next 24 hours. Yet Jesus counters this errant thinking with the question, "Is not life more important than food, and the body more important than clothes?" (v. 25). Priorities should not be determined by immediacy but rather longevity; not by what will come first, but what lasts the longest.

Although we may feel we are solely responsible for our existence, we are not. "Your heavenly Father knows that you need [all these things]" (v. 32). This expression shares that we are not in this alone. We wrongly put more emphasis on independence than dependence.

Jesus reassures us that our dilemma between independence with creation and allegiance to God is understood by the One who placed us here. We are assured of

His provision. Jesus used several illustrations from nature to illustrate how God provides, and that He will even more generously care for us, whom He greatly loves. We are tempted to prioritize our own resources above dependence on God, yet Jesus assures us that the Father knows and provides for us as we trust in Him.

Although we may feel torn between two differing demands, there is only one: "Seek first his kingdom and his righteousness, and all these things will be given to you as well" (v. 33). Some years ago on a television show, a private detective was caught in a rather desperate situation. He had entered an area that was guarded by a large, nasty dog. Having been discovered by the canine, the hero ran back to his car so as not to become mauled. However, with the dog running swiftly toward him, he arrived at his car only to discover he had locked the door. Fighting panic, he reached into his pocket and retrieved his keys. Aware of the fast-approaching guard dog, he concentrated on his fumbling hands with the keys while repeatedly mumbling to himself, "Unlock the door. Don't look at the dog." If he had concentrated on the most threatening issue at the time, it would have been the dog, but that would not have brought him safety. The same is true with us, our priorities should not be determined by what is the most threatening, but rather what is to our ultimate good.

These three teachings of Jesus might help us in determining how we are to relate to the creation and its Creator, but there is still the danger of extremes. Humanity seldom does anything in moderation. We pass over the middle ground in favor of one excess or another.

These extremes are expressed in a number of ways within our dilemma.

Who's Responsible?

If we accept that God provides for us, as Jesus said, does this leave us without responsibility? On one extreme we have those who say, "God helps those who help them-selves." As the old saying goes, "God may feed the birds, but He doesn't drop the worms in the nest." On the other extreme are those that believe human effort is a statement against faith.

While attending college and seminary, I encountered individuals who were attending solely by the belief that God had called them and would provide for their needs. Their tuition and living expenses materialized from a num-ber of unknown sources. Although they were often uncer-tain of their future, many made it through. I, however, did not feel so directed. My tuition, rent, and food came from both my wife and I working. Does this mean that God pro-vided for the others and not for me? No. God provided for all of us, just through differing means. The jobs I held while studying were unmistakably given to me by God.

All of us are at different levels of experience, requiring different care by God. I am sure those who spent their years studying without need of employment are busily em-ployed within their respective ministries now. There may be a day when circumstances may limit my productivity, and I will need to wait on God to provide through other means. In either case, God still provides. The issue that must be determined is not whether we are specifically pas-sive or active at any one time, but rather where are we in God's leading. Our primary task is to seek the kingdom of God and His righteousness. We are assured of God's pro-vision to His faithful ones in this, though the source of these provisions varies. After all, there were times when Jesus fed His disciples by miraculous means (John 6:1-13), and there were times when they plucked the heads of grain as they walked along (Matthew 12:1).

How Much Is Enough?

Another topic of extremes falls under the question, "How much is enough?" Where do "needs" end and "wants" begin? Jesus assures us that God knows our needs and supplies them. Paul echoes this in Philippians 4:19. But what are necessities and what are wants? In a society based heavily upon materialism, this distinction can be difficult. Yesterday's excess is today's necessity. Think about it! How easily could you get along without your microwave, dishwasher, automatic washer, or television remote? These items, rather recent in their development, are already considered necessities in many homes.

Some would determine necessity based upon the individual items, but the determination appears to be more general—our reason for possession. Again we apply the dictum of Jesus, "Seek first his kingdom and his righteousness." By applying this to our reason for possession, whatever the item might be, its necessity is determined by how it enables our quest. Possessions for possessions' sake can be dangerously distracting. Possessions for the Kingdom's sake can be fulfilling.

I have encountered two extremes to this idea during my ministry. One was a dear saintly lady in a congregation I formerly served. Visiting her home, you might think she was impoverished. She drove an older car, had wood floors instead of carpet, and lived a plain existence without many of the luxuries we are accustomed to seeing in homes. However, her lifestyle did not reflect her financial position. While she was not a wealthy woman, she spent little on herself so that she could contribute to God's ministry. On the other hand, in my present congregation, there is an ordained minister who owns a number of cars, trucks, motorcycles, snowmobiles, and so forth. Some might look at his possessions and question what influence is motivating him in service to God. However, his ministry is unique. He spends his life ministering at motorcycle rallies, rodeos, horseback trails, and snowmobile weekends across the nation. His possessions are actually tools of his trade, and because of them, many people are exposed to the gospel who otherwise would not be.

Whether it is appropriate to own something cannot be determined by the item itself, but by how that item encourages or detracts us from our pilgrimage with God. A popular saying among people today is, "The one who dies with the most toys wins." But we must also add, "The one who dies with the most toys still dies." Here is the real issue: What do I own that moves me toward God's kingdom and righteousness? What do I own that draws me away? In answering these questions, we begin to discern necessity from desire. As Paul told the Corinthians, "'Everything is permissible'—but not everything is beneficial" (1 Corinthians 10:23).

How Much to Produce?

A third area of extreme deals with production. One could argue that the manufacture of things we only *want* is as wrong as possessing them. The evil is found in the tedious balance we maintain between production and consumption. The issue is a vicious circle. In order for us to purchase items, we must possess the means of purchase, usually money. To earn this money, we are usually employed. If the worker produces more goods than can be consumed by the public, sales taper off and the manufacturer begins to lose money. To protect against losses, the manufacturer cuts expenses by laying off the work force, reducing production. Thus a careful control must be maintained. Too much production or too little consumption and the balance is lost.

To aid in this balance, two dangerous influences have been developed—unnecessary consumption and overspending. Many of the products being manufactured today could be taken from our shelves and the human race would continue quite well. In fact, many of the items are sold first by *creating* a market for them. Manufacturers must convince us that their products are something we need to have. Here enters the advertisement industry, whose sole purpose is to attract our attention to a product and convince us that life would be impossible without it. The success of this approach is obvious in the number of items in existence that we really do not need.

However, even the best advertisements cannot overcome our ability to produce more than we can consume. This challenge is answered in two other ways: Either make a percentage of our producers idle or enable consumers to consume more. Mostly we opt for the second alternative.

Increasing consumerism is done by increasing the ability to purchase items manufactured. The most popular way of increasing buying power today is through credit cards. Plastic enables many of us to consume items that we normally could not afford to buy. We can have it now, as long as we agree to make small payments each month to the lending agency, which is rewarded for its generosity by a significant finance charge. We know how dangerous this experience can be. Credit cards and loans are far easier to obtain than pay off, setting new records each year for accumulated debt in our society.

The extremes of this dilemma are found between those who would advocate self-denial and those who promote consumption. Some see the vast array of goods and the ability to experience them as a blessing of God to be enjoyed. Others see them as an evil trap that entangles us in our self-made snares. The common ground between these two could be expressed, "It is not how many possessions we have, but how many possessions have us." Are we living for the kingdom of God or an earthly kingdom? Who convinces us of our need for an item—actors in humorous advertisements or the Holy Spirit?

It is not the item that we possess that is the problem, but the effect of that item on our relationship with God. If it is not making the Kingdom alive to us or producing a deepened righteousness, then it is suspect. Could our present social predicaments be seen as a reflection of a people less interested in the kingdom of God and more concerned with creation itself? If we allowed Jesus' challenge of priority to lead us, would we be as caught up in this vicious circle?

One final consideration is the resultant impact our consumer-driven economy has on our environment. Whether it be the natural resources we use in the items' manufacture, operation, and eventual disposal, everything we produce and consume comes at an expense to the creation we have been placed within. The pendulum swing goes from those who say creation was placed here to be expended for humanity's enjoyment to those who believe we are to be responsible stewards of all God gave us.

Conclusion

How then do we respond to the dilemma of serving the Creator and not creation? By keeping our focus on the kingdom of God and His righteousness. Remember, all other benefits and experiences received from our interaction with creation pales in comparison to these two great gifts of the Father. No other aspect of creation will continue into the realms to which these realities will take us. If our relationship to creation is consistently viewed in light of God's kingdom and righteousness, the balance will be kept and the dilemma resolved.

Background Scripture: Genesis 1:26, 28-30; 2:7-9; Matthew 5—7; 12:1; John 1:1, 3; 6:1-13; 14:3; 17:13-21; Philippians 4:19

About the Author: Rev. Mark A. Holmes is senior pastor of Darrow Road Wesleyan Church in Superior, Wisconsin.

At Issue: *How much are humans able to do in their own efforts? Are humans wrong in creating creature comforts? Are humans "playing God" in such areas as genetics, medical reesearch, and so forth?*

Common Ground: *God has given us gifts, talents, and abilities, and we are responsible to use them wisely.*

CHAPTER 5

Human Effort

by Mark A. Holmes

As it is with many decisions, Eve had no idea how influential her choice in the Garden would be. More than a daily grocery store determination between grapes on sale or oranges that look good, Eve's choice would have a universal impact. She thought she had understood what God had told her concerning the fruit she was being tempted to enjoy. But then, she was informed she would not die. Instead, she would become like God, knowing the difference between good and evil. The enticement of a new ability would prove too much. Desiring the pleasure and fulfillment promised by the act, she bit into the fruit in full anticipation. Likewise, Adam sought the same pleasure, and together they are the first of all humanity to discern right from wrong.

The serpent of the account did not lie about their new potential. They *were* enabled to differentiate good from evil. What the serpent failed to mention was, having an ability and exercising it properly are two different things. They became able to distinguish between good and evil. However, they, like us, could no longer control the outcomes of their choice.

From that decision on, humanity has been continually challenged by its ability and inability to live within creation. The appropriate exercise of our capabilities is often the subject of long debates within the Church. Yet, at least, the source of our enablement is *common ground*. Being natural and supernatural in essence, our abilities, gifts, and talents come from God, enabling us to face the challenges of our natural and supernatural environments.

Our natural abilities stem from creation itself. Being formed by God from the substance of the earth (Genesis 2:7), we were given certain abilities to relate and interact with the world. Yet, our natural capabilities extend beyond those simple actions most associated with survival to those empowerments that raise us to a level above the rest of creation. Scripturally, this is expressed as being created in God's image (1:26). This image is not physical in nature. Instead, it is expressed in the abilities to love, reason, create, appreciate beauty, plan ahead, recognize the holy, and so forth. All are God-given distinctives that are not found in the other less nobly made creatures. Because of these, we are able to relate to creation, one another, and God. We can do a number of things that others of creation find impossible. The natural abilities were given to enable humanity to maintain its created place within this world as caretaker and overseer (vv. 28-30; 2:15).

As wonderful as these natural abilities are, they are not sufficient for the challenges facing humankind. True, we have been created from the dust of the ground (2:7), as were the other creatures (v. 19). However, humans were blessed with an extra feature; God breathed into us a life force that we refer to as our soul (v. 7). This ensoulment places us as participants within two worlds: the natural (within creation) and the supernatural (beyond creation). Each environment has its unique challenges requiring our reliance upon different God-given abilities. Challenges from within creation can be quite difficult, but challenges from beyond creation stretch us beyond our human or natural means.

Paul refers to this supernatural challenge in Ephesians 6:10-20. He tells us our battle is not against natural enemies made of flesh and blood, but against the supernatural rulers, powers, forces of darkness, and spiritual forces of evil. To battle these, God has given His followers an "armor" made up of truth, righteousness, the gospel of peace, faith, salvation, God's Word, and prayer. All of these are useful means through which we can exercise our God-given tendencies.

In addition to this armor, God has also enabled us through the Holy Spirit. This empowerment is apparent through three different influences. The first of these is the presence of the Holy Spirit himself. For example, Jesus tells us the Holy Spirit will become our Counselor (John 14:16). We are reassured of God's indwelling within His followers in the person of the Holy Spirit (v. 23). The Holy Spirit will remind us of Christ's teachings (v. 26). He will also guide us into all truth, disclose the future, and reveal God's will to us (16:13-14). Jesus would later reassure His disciples at His ascension that they would receive power when the Holy Spirit came upon them, enabling them to become His witnesses (Acts 1:8). Christians believe the power of the Holy Spirit enables us to face the challenges of our supernatural experience.

A second empowerment by the Holy Spirit is experienced through what Paul referred to as "fruit of the Spirit" (Galatians 5:22-23). These are the supernatural heightening of emotions, enabling a more complete expression. The emotions—love, joy, peace, patience, kindness, goodness, faithfulness, gentleness, and self control—are expressed in their pure form, resulting not *from* our experiences of life but often *in spite of* these experiences.

The empowerment of the Holy Spirit is also demonstrated through certain abilities Paul refers to as "gifts, according to the grace given us" (Romans 12:6). While their exact expression and usage is sometimes a controversial issue within the Church, their source and purpose are generally agreed upon. In a list in Romans 12:7-8, Paul explains these enablements are extensions of God's grace toward us, to be used in bringing a unified fruitfulness to

Christ's Body, the Church. His description in 1 Corinthians 12:7-10, develops a unity-through-diversity theme. Each person exercising the gifts given to him or her develops a unified expression within the Church. He also emphasizes that these gifts are given to us by the Holy Spirit. Finally, in Ephesians 4:11, Paul credits this gifting to Jesus, for the purpose of preparing God's people for service and developing their spiritual maturity. Some of the gifts given to us by God include healing, prophecy, faith, teaching, discernment, pastoring, speaking in languages, interpretation of languages, miracles, mercy, and evangelism.

God has been more than generous in supplying His followers with an abundance of abilities by which we can live in this world, fulfilling His desires for us and creation. However, we still face the challenge of sin introduced by Adam and Eve. When they made that fateful decision to become wise like God, they plummeted humanity into a state of depravity limiting us in every area of life. This challenges humanity in the proper use of abilities. While God has given them for our good, our depraved nature can use them to our detriment. This misuse can be divided into two basic expressions: sins of commission (what we do) and sins of omission (what we fail to do). Thus, using our abilities incorrectly or failing to use them as we should results in sin.

In Genesis 11:1-9, we find a classic illustration of humanity's sin by commission. The account of the Tower of Babel stands as a monument to the human error of exercising our abilities over dependence upon God. By common agreement, the people set to work on a rather aggressive building project. They would build a city and a large tower that would extend to heaven. Building cities and towers are not sinful actions. It is what motivated this building that made their efforts wrong. We are told they wanted to make a name for themselves and reach heaven (v. 4). These desires attempt to usurp God's authority and position. It describes two basic tendencies of our fallen nature: to replace God with humanity and take control. Instead of being known as a creation of God, the Babel builders would become known for what they had created. They would take the initiative and even storm heaven by their abilities. However, God intervened in their endeavor by limiting one of His previously given attributes—communication. Prior to this, a common language was used among all people. By changing this common language, understanding and cooperation broke down, making their project impossible.

The reason for God's intervention was not the insecurity of a superior fearful of being overtaken. Instead, God assessed that humanity was sacrificing dependency in favor of ability, which would result in greater problems. Dependency and ability are usually viewed as opposites in a spectrum. Our motivation is to live by developing the latter and lessen the former. We spend the first half of our lives striving to obtain independence and the latter half struggling to retain it. Thus, dependency is often viewed as an obstacle to human ability. Yet, ability can never be totally devoid of dependence because of sin and human frailty. Our nature makes us unable to comprehend all the ramifications of any particular action. At best, our foresight is cloudy. Thus every aspect of human endeavor, no matter how noble, is limited. We may have abilities, but we are still dependent on God for realizing their proper exercise. When we push dependence aside in favor of our own ability, our actions can become distorted and twisted. When we act within the sphere of God's influence, our abilities can take on a more accurate expression.

Our continued desire to storm heaven and make a name for ourselves has cost us in the past. Like Eve, we still want to be like God. The problem is, we have never fully mastered what it means to be human. So, we exercise our abilities, influenced by our sinful errors, sometimes to our advancement and other times to our detriment.

Luke 19:11-26 brings us to the sin of omission. It is a parable shared by Jesus that illustrates both the provision and expectation given to humanity by God. Before the master leaves, he distributes among his servants various amounts of money to be used in his absence. When the master returns, he calls his servants together to inquire as to the fruitfulness of his gifts. Two servants are faithful in their work, producing not only the original gift but an additional amount. The third servant comes with only the gift, having carefully protected it from loss by hiding it away. The first two are rewarded for their commission. The latter is condemned for his omission.

The error of the nonproductive servant was not sloth as much as caution. He feared the misuse of the talent would result in its loss. God's indictment of the slave was for his failure to use what had been given him. With God's empowerment of humanity comes a number of expectations in which it is to be used. Making disciples, loving one another, caring for those in need, worshiping God, teaching and leading, living exemplary lives, caring for the world, and many other activities become the responsibility of those who would claim Christ as Savior. Yet, the potential of a sinful use of these abilities leave some hesitant to exercise them.

Here, then, is one of the great dilemmas facing humanity. To exercise our God-given abilities could result in a negative effect. To not use our abilities could allow existing problems to go unchecked. Proponents of the first view cry out for restraint, while those for the latter stress activity. What should be done? How shall it be done? The history of humanity illustrates a number of attempts we have made to answer these questions, both to our advancement and detriment.

Alfred Nobel invented dynamite. He believed its potential use would be a help to humanity. However, its power was soon utilized in warfare, becoming a means of destruction. Disheartened by this, he directed that his estate should be used to encourage peace and the advancement of humanity. Today, the world still rewards those individuals who contribute most to humanity's good with the Nobel Peace Prize.

For years, the insecticide known as DDT was used for the control of insects within the agricultural community. This great development of humanity was presented as the greatest weapon in our arsenal against crop destruction. However, because of our limited foresight, we could not completely perceive the other effects this chemical would have in our world. Eventually, we realized that DDT was not only effective in poisoning insects but also birds, animals, and humans.

Today, one of our main controversies is found in genetics. Scientists have developed abilities to manipulate the structure of cells to influence the most basic forces of life. Whether it be the cloning of sheep or the restructuring of plants to produce their own natural pesticide or become frost resistant, we continually develop abilities without the benefit of knowing what their complete impact on life will be.

New abilities are developed every day, and with them comes the question of not just "Can we?" but "Should we?" Just because we can do something, does it mean it should be done? On the other hand, God gave us the ability to do the things we do. Are we to deny our God-given potential? Does ability take precedence over propriety? What about the correctness of the act, its moral and ethical impact? What about the need of the endeavor to heal a disease or feed the world? These considerations become the great check-and-balance system of human endeavor.

Human ability raises the question of morality, and with it, the potential of building a figurative Tower of Babel. How do we determine the correctness of any act? Some would contend from utility. The ability to do something argues for its use. Others base their reasoning on pragmatism. Does it get the job done? There are those who base their propriety on emotivism. Does it feel good or heighten one's enjoyment in life? Others argue from compassion. If we can, we must! Basic to all these views and others is the underlying question of what is good, proper, and moral. Is it based upon the activity itself or on a higher standard? In an effort to answer this question, humankind has developed a number of views that have served to move us closer to God or farther away, depending upon the position held. In some cases we have built our own philosophical towers and cities, defining what is right and wrong. In other cases we have drawn a new appreciation for the dependence on God needed to live in this world, exercising His abilities.

A thought often expressed during this consideration of abilities comes as either a question or an indictment: "Are we playing God?" In one sense, everything we do as humans is "playing God" since it is His very attributes that enable us to function. I am playing God by writing words of reason on a piece of paper. You are playing God by reading them and contemplating their meaning. Even Jesus told His disciples that they would do greater things than He.

The idea of playing God is often expressed as a negative, implying we may be overstepping our bounds. However, the negative is not found so much in the ability as in the level of dependence we exercise within the act. If our development of abilities and influences are done in dependence upon God's direction and control, we are using them as God intended. If we neglect God's leading, then we build human towers and, with them, human error and its repercussions. The fact that God has given us our abilities, patterned after His own, implies that we will inevitably be involved in activities associated with His. Thus the question is not, "Are we playing God?" but rather, "What would God have us play?"

Bishop Wright was incensed in response to a vision-ary who spoke during a church conference on the possibil-ity that one day humans would develop the ability to fly. Proclaiming his disagreement to the gathering that God never intended humans to take to the air, he gathered his two sons, Orville and Wilbur, and left the assembly. Where would we be today if the sons had embraced their father's view? As the two brothers, working from their bicy-cle shop and later on the beach at Kitty Hawk, wrestled with the intricacies of aerodynamics, did they play God?

So what is our answer? How do we accurately address this dilemma, considering our limitations and our needs? Perhaps we should look to Jesus, the One who lived with-in this creation, empowered by God to do all things, and yet never performed anything not in keeping with His Fa-ther's will. What type of motives challenged Jesus to act? It is easy to list a number of these: love, compassion, em-pathy, justice, and mercy. These drive us as well. How did He keep them in check?

The apostle Paul, in Philippians 2:6-8, outlines the at-titude of Jesus that we, as images of God, are to have in our exercise of abilities. Though made in the nature of God, we are not to seek equality. Though set in a position of supremacy within the world, we are to take a servant's place. Though being elevated because of our God-given abilities, we must recognize our dependence with humility.

By these, we become the tools through which God can work, to care for a world and people distorted by sin. By having this same attitude that existed in Jesus, we can be faithful to appropriately "play God" in this world, exer-cising the very image He created within us, without dis-torting or destroying creation in the process.

Although separated by millennia, we are not much different than Eve. As she stood contemplating in the Gar-den of Eden, so we also stand in the face of our challenges and abilities. The choice is ours, as will be the effects of each decision. What will determine the outcome will be the voice we choose to heed in making the decision.

Background Scripture: Genesis 1:26, 28-30; 2:7, 15, 19; 11:1-9; Luke 19:11-26; John 14:16, 23; 16:13-14; Acts 1:8; Romans 12:6-8; 1 Corinthians 12:7-10; Galatians 5:22-23; Ephesians 4:11; 6:10-20; Philippians 2:6-8

About the Author: Rev. Mark A. Holmes is senior pastor of Darrow Road Wesleyan Church in Superior, Wisconsin.

At Issue: *Do the biblical concepts of kings and rulers apply to governments of today? How are Christians expected to relate to modern governments?*

Common Ground: *The ideal is for government to act like a shepherd to the people. The reality is it often does not act that way.*

CHAPTER 6

The Purpose of Government

by Karl Martin

Historically, the Christian church has affirmed the legitimacy of civil government. Christians, that is, have acknowledged that civil authorities have the right to rule the nations of this earth. The purpose of this chapter is to review the most significant biblical passages regarding the role of government and to reflect on how modern ideas about government have changed the ways Christians think about the purpose of government.

The Purposes of Government in the Old Testament

The most natural place to begin a review of the biblical passages concerning civil government is with those passages related to the children of Israel in the Promised Land, for it was there that the children of Israel first had the authority to create their own government. As recounted in the Books of Joshua and Judges, Joshua led the people as they conquered the Promised Land and divided the land among the tribes of Israel. Following the death of Joshua, another form of government developed; it was a loosely established system of judges who acted, in some way or another, for God. Some of these judges, such as Deborah and Gideon, were also the spiritual leaders of the people. Others—Samson provides the clearest example—

were political but not spiritual leaders. While this system of judges allowed a leader inspired by God to rise to a place of influence, it was not to last.

The first turning point in the history of the government of God's chosen people is recorded in the eighth chapter of 1 Samuel. Samuel had grown old, and his sons had been appointed as the judges over Israel. His sons, seduced by power and wealth, became corrupt and were no longer serving the best interest of the people. In response to the corruption, the older members of the tribes came to Samuel and asked him to appoint a king over them.

Samuel, naturally, took the matter to God in prayer. God responded by telling Samuel to go ahead and listen to the people, but God made it clear to Samuel that He considered the request an affront. The people of Israel decided that they no longer wanted God to rule over them directly. God, through Samuel, warned the people just what they could expect from a king. In spite of Samuel's warning, the people continued to insist on having a king. By reviewing why the people wished to have a king and by reviewing God's warning through Samuel concerning kings, we learn a great deal about what we might and might not expect from our own forms of government.

The most commonly known reason given by the children of Israel for wanting a king was so that they might be like other nations. The Book of 1 Samuel, however, is more specific. The children of Israel did not merely want to be like other nations. They wanted a king because he would rule over them, lead them, and fight their battles for them (8:20). We can certainly understand why God might consider a request for such a monarch an affront.

God's warnings are also very instructive to us. God warned the people that the king would draft their young men into military service, require the labor of their sons and daughters for his own benefit, and tax their abundance. In spite of all these warnings—and they all prove significant over and over again in the history of the children of Israel—they continued to desire a king, and God granted them their request.

What can we learn from the establishment of the monarchy as recounted in 1 Samuel? Perhaps we can learn that it is the purpose of government to tax the people and spend those resources. The taxes may take the form of a tax on wealth, property, or labor. Whatever form they take, they are taxes nonetheless. And the spending will most certainly include allocations for military projects. In addition, the spending will probably include money allocated to allow the government to continue. Under a monarchy, this may mean money distributed by the monarch to his or her officials. Under other forms of government, this may mean money distributed to establish and maintain a bureaucracy whose agencies are designed to carry out government programs.

These practices are not condemned by God through Samuel. They are simply presented as what the people should expect. The history of the kings of Israel recorded elsewhere in the Old Testament teaches us that people might also expect governments to be prone to corruption. The story of Rehoboam, recorded in 1 Kings 12:1-19, provides a striking example of corruption and its implications. While the collection of taxes and the spending of public resources for the common good and for the maintenance of the government are presented as expectations in 1 Samuel, Rehoboam's story teaches us that those with power within a government may abuse it. Following Solomon's death, his son Rehoboam succeeded him. Jeroboam led a group who felt that Solomon had mistreated them and appealed to Rehoboam for relief. Rejecting the advice of his older advisers, Rehoboam promised, not to lighten the load placed on the people by Solomon, but to increase it. As the story illustrates, it is certainly possible for those in power in a government to reject the appropriate role of government and use the power of the government to further their personal goals. In Rehoboam's case, he appeared more concerned with looking tough to his younger advisers than with fairly exercising the purpose of the government.

The result of the decision of the children of Israel to seek a king had significant, long-term implications. Eventually, in part because of poor choices of leaders like Rehoboam, the children of Israel came to be ruled over by outsiders. In other words, God's chosen ones came to be ruled over by those who were not chosen by God. This situation continued into the Jewish world at the time described in the New Testament. With this background, we can look briefly at the purpose of government at the time of the writing of the New Testament.

The Purposes of Government in the New Testament

At the time of the birth of Jesus, the Jewish people had lived and practiced their faith under the political domination of non-Jewish people for the better part of 500 years. While they experienced some periods of political autonomy, the basic experience of the Jewish people was that of a people serving a foreign government. Christianity, therefore, emerged in a world very different from the one described in the books of history included in the Old Testament. The idea of a theocracy, a society ruled directly by God (perhaps patterned after the period of the judges) is far in the background for New Testament writers.

The Christian believers of whom we learn in the New Testament provide us with a very different view of the purpose of government than their Jewish counterparts in the Old Testament, for Christians never formed a nation the way their Jewish counterparts did. Therefore, Christians most often wrote about what it meant to be both a Christian and a citizen of a non-Christian state. In addition, much of the New Testament reflects the belief that history is running out, that Christ will soon return. Few New Testament writers, it seems, would have envisioned that Christians 20 centuries later would be looking to them for guidance and information about the purpose of government.

The apostle Paul and other New Testament writers assume that the believer will have what amounts to a dual citizenship. For Paul this meant he was simultaneously a Roman citizen and a Christian. Often this was not a problem—the demands of his citizenship did not conflict with his Christian faith. At times his Roman citizenship actually worked to his advantage, gaining him fair treatment he would not have received were he not a Roman citizen. Such is the case with the imprisonment of Paul and Silas recorded in Acts 16. But at times the demands of the faith and the responsibilities to political authorities came into conflict. While the political authorities in the story are members of the Sanhedrin, a religious body, and not the Romans, the story of the response of Peter and John recorded in Acts 4 provides one example of early Christians responding to this tension. Peter and John said, "Judge for yourselves whether it is right in God's sight to obey you rather than God" (Acts 4:19). The confrontation between Peter and John and the members of the Sanhedrin provides a model for the kinds of confrontations Christians will feel at times with those in authority over nations or institutions. How are Christians to know when it is appropriate to listen to God rather than those in authority? How are Christians to know when a government is exercising its appropriate purpose? That question has led Christians through the years to the writings of the apostle Paul's letter to the Romans.

Paul's Letter to the Romans

At first glance, Paul's instructions in Romans 13 seem to allow for no compromise:

> Everyone must submit himself to the governing authorities, for there is no authority except that which God has established. The authorities that exist have been established by God *(v. 1)*.

> For rulers hold no terror for those who do right, but for those who do wrong. Do you want to be free from fear of the one in authority? Then do what is right and he will commend you *(v. 3)*.

Yet we can immediately think of historical situations when Paul's admonition has not turned out that way. Certainly a Christian in Nazi Germany who harbored a Jewish friend would have been doing the right thing in the judgment of most Christians today, yet that same Christian would certainly have had much to fear from the government. We could cite many other examples. What are we to make of Paul's advice in light of what history has taught us? As is usually the case, the text itself offers us insight.

Romans 12 offers insights that help us place Paul's comments about authority in perspective. He wrote, "Love must be sincere. Hate what is evil; cling to what is good" (v. 9). He also wrote, "If it is possible, as far as it depends on you, live at peace with everyone" (v. 18). How are we to reconcile these verses with what we find in chapter 13? Certainly no easy answer exists, but the context of chapter 12 undoubtedly keeps us from reading what Paul wrote in chapter 13 as the final word on the subject. In light of what Paul wrote, it would not be fair to say that Paul merely believed it is the purpose of government to be obeyed because its authority is God ordained.

Paul's own experiences and behavior in relationship to authority also provide us with insight. Certainly Paul was not willing to grant authority to the Sanhedrin when its members had him arrested in Jerusalem. On that occasion Paul used the authority of the Roman state to counteract the actions of the Jewish leaders. Had he followed the instructions given in Romans 13:1 to the letter, Paul would have had no basis for challenging the authority of the Sanhedrin.

So the New Testament shows us Christians living in the same tension we experience today. They recognized the authority of civil and religious bodies as a general rule. That is, they acknowledged the authority over them when they could because one of the purposes of government is to maintain order in a society. But they also recognized that there were times when, to do the will of God, they had to disobey authority. How could they, and how can we, know when to obey and when not to obey? Neither the Bible, nor Christian tradition, nor our own personal experience can give us a final answer we might apply to every circumstance. Still, all three can help us think more clearly about the issue.

Christians and Democratic Forms of Government

The rise of more democratic forms of government in the modern world have only added a layer of complexity to the issue. For, in a democracy, the people are responsible not only *to* the government but also *for* the government. That is, citizens in a democracy have the power to alter the character of the very government they are instructed to obey. Monarchs in the past have claimed to rule by divine authority, but government officials elected by a popular majority have a much more difficult time making such a claim. After all, we know the exact percentages of the vote each candidate earned. It is one thing to say with Paul that a ruler has authority only because he or she has been granted authority by God when he or she is

a monarch and his or her family's rise to power is shroud-
ed in mystery for most of his or her subjects. It is another
thing to say that a president, senator, or congressional rep-
resentative rules with the authority of God when we know
he or she could be voted out of office in the next election.
Or, for example, if we believe that a president is in office
by the will of God, what right have we to work to defeat
that same president running for reelection? We still may
wish to affirm that those who rule in authority over us rule
by the authority of God, but democratic elections have
forced us to rethink the issues.

Summary

What then, from a biblical perspective, is the purpose
of government? One purpose is to maintain order, to re-
strain those who would infringe on the rights of others. We
see this purpose expressed in the life of the apostle Paul
when he appeals to the Roman government to mediate between him and the members of the Sanhedrin. Another
purpose of government is to collect taxes and allocate resources. This is what God, through Samuel, tells the children of Israel their government (their king) will do. Because of these legitimate roles, governments are to be
respected and obeyed when, in good conscience, Christians can do so. However, the Bible also provides certain
warnings to Christians concerning governments.

Governments are likely to turn aside from their legitimate purposes and begin to act in the best interest of the
monarch or a ruling elite rather than in the best interest of
the people. Governments may, for example, tax unfairly or
allocate resources inappropriately. Governments may also
become the oppressive agent in a society when their appropriate purpose would be to protect citizens from such
oppressive agents.

So, identifying the purpose of government is not
enough. Christians in democratic societies, in societies

where citizens have the right to alter their form of government, need to reflect on appropriate ways to interact with their governments. For the biblical record seems to indicate whatever the purpose of government is, that purpose will be distorted at times.

Background Scripture: 1 Samuel 8; 1 Kings 12:1-19; Acts 4:19; Romans 12:9, 18; 13:1, 3

About the Author: Dr. Martin holds a Ph.D. in American Studies from the University of Minnesota. He teaches in the Department of Literature, Journalism, and Modern Languages at Point Loma Nazarene University.

At Issue: *Is the Church a change agent for government? Should Christians run for public office? Is the purpose of democracy to establish a Christian nation or to guarantee that we are free to practice the religion of our choice?*

Common Ground: *Government is meant to allow us to live "peaceful and quiet lives in all godliness and holiness" (1 Timothy 2:2).*

CHAPTER 7

Christians in Government

by Karl Martin

Backed by fairly clear biblical support, Christians can agree that they have a responsibility to pray for those in authority over them and, under most circumstances, submit to civil authorities. Beyond this, many Christians would also agree that responsible involvement in government is appropriate. Still, when it comes to what is and what is not responsible involvement, Christians have honest differences of opinion. Should Christians vote? Should they run for public office? Should they serve in wars? Should they protest against policies they believe are unjust? Should they allow themselves to be arrested? Should they even resort to armed resistance against oppressive forces? At various times in history, men and women who identify themselves as Christians have answered both yes and no to all of these questions.

The Legacy of the Puritans in America

When American Christians reflect on the Christian role in government, they often return to the Puritans, for the Puritans thought carefully about this issue and have much to offer us as we reflect on our world today. Yet, much has changed since the days of the Massachusetts Bay Colony, and, if we are not careful, we can distort the legacy left to us by the Puritans.

While the Puritans certainly came to America in search of religious freedom for themselves, they were not interested in extending that religious freedom to others. Within the boundaries of the colony, they hoped to establish a theocracy, a society ruled by God. For the Puritans, civil and religious authority were united; consequently, religious dissenters were also seen as threats to civil stability. People such as Anne Hutchinson, Roger Williams, and the Quakers were sometimes banished from the colony because of their divergent religious beliefs. Few Christians in the modern world would want to return to a society so strictly defined, but the Puritan standards of devotion and citizenship will always remain an inspiration to many Christians.

Even Christians as devout as the Puritans had trouble sustaining their God-centered society. With the second and third generations, Puritan leaders faced a dilemma. Christian behavior was being expected of those who could not give testimony of Christian conversion. Because the Puritans believed that those who would be saved were "elected" for salvation by God, they could not expect that all citizens born in the colony would be among the elect. True discipleship could not be forced, and Christian behavior was not likely to come from those not among the elect. This caused great tension within Puritan families and within Puritan society.

A significant portion of the legacy of the Puritans for us is this question: Can Christian morality precede Christian conversion? If not, is it fair to establish laws that reflect Christian morality? Within the world of politics, the question is often posed this way: Can we legislate morality?

Heaven on Earth?

At the start of *The Scarlet Letter,* a classic novel set in Puritan New England, Nathaniel Hawthorne wrote:

> The founders of a new colony, whatever Utopia of human virtue and happiness they might originally

project, have invariably recognized it among their earliest practical necessities to allot a portion of the virgin soil as a cemetery, and another as the site of the prison.[1]

Hawthorne's point is that a gulf exists between what human beings strive to create and what they are actually able to create. This is an insight the Puritans certainly would have understood.

It is an insight we must understand as well. For, no matter how hard we try, we will never be able to establish God's kingdom in all its fullness on earth before Christ's return. This should not depress us or discourage our involvement, but it should make us cautious and thoughtful. Our involvement in politics and government should always be done in the awareness that whatever good we can accomplish will pale in comparison to the beauty of God's kingdom.

Christians should have another reason to be cautious about their involvement with politics. Modern nations often intermingle nationalism and calls for reform. When Italians are called to be "real" Italians, or Germans are called to be "real" Germans, we can be sure that some group will be identified as "other" and made to pay the price for corrupting a "pure" society. The same can be said for nationalism in America. When Christians remember that they are Christians first and members of a modern nation second, they will be hesitant to become too involved in nationalistic causes. After all, as a Christian I have brothers and sisters in Christ in every nation on the planet. I wouldn't want them to come to harm from a government acting in my name. With so much complexity facing us as we think about Christian political involvement, we might be tempted to simply withdraw from politics altogether. Certainly this is not what the gospel would lead us to do.

The Transforming Power of the Gospel

Christians know that the gospel has the power to transform the lives of people. After all, Christians themselves have been transformed. That transformative power can work at the level of the individual or the group. We have seen families and churches transformed by the power of the gospel. Might the gospel transform cities, states, and even nations? We would be selling the power of the gospel short if we said it could not. So most Christians remain committed to trying to spread the influence of the gospel through involvement in the civil life of their cities, states, and nations.

Of course, we should always keep in mind that when we are doing politics, we are not necessarily doing the work of the kingdom of God. Still, the work we do in the political realm can make the work of the kingdom of God more effective. With all this in mind, we can turn to various forms of participation and examine both their promises and their dangers.

Voting

Voting is the most fundamental right of a citizen in a democracy; thus, it is the most basic way for the Christian to interact with his or her government. Certainly, if we believe that the mind of the Christian is being molded to resemble the mind of Christ, we would want the Christian to express his or her preferences regarding laws and leaders in his or her society by voting.

Yet some Christians would object even to voting, and we must not dismiss their objections too quickly. Some Christians might believe that by voting we are participating in worldly power structures, we are involving ourselves in secular matters rather than solely working to build the kingdom of God. Other Christians would counter this point of view by saying that, although by voting we are not necessarily advancing the Kingdom, if we do not vote, we remove Christian influence from the political system. It is probably safe to say that most Christians would consider a prayerful vote as the duty of the citizen who is a Christian.

But is voting enough? If we believe that the votes we cast as Christians reflect our understanding of the will of God for our day and situation, can we content ourselves with voting only? In his famous essay, "On the Duty of Civil Disobedience," Henry David Thoreau wrote this about voting:

> I cast my vote, perchance, as I think right; but I am not vitally concerned that the right should prevail. I am willing to leave it to the majority. . . . Even voting for the right is doing nothing for it. It is only expressing to men feebly your desire that it should prevail.[2]

Many Christians would agree with Thoreau and feel that Christians should do more than just vote. Christians with the interest and resources should consider running for office.

Running for Office

Christians who feel that voting alone is not a strongly engaged enough response to the issue often either run for office themselves or encourage other Christians to run for office. Candidates for local school boards and candidates for the presidency have sometimes acknowledged that their primary motivation for running for office is their faith. As a greater involvement in the political process, running for office not only promises greater influence but also contains greater risks. We will examine both the positive and negative aspects in turn.

Obviously, elected officials can have greater influence than voters in general elections. Elected officials have the responsibility for the creation of policy; thus, they can avoid the limited potential given to voting by Thoreau. Now we see that Christians can much more directly form laws and social programs consistent with the values of the gospel. If a single Christian elected official can make a difference, consider what a number of Christians might do if they served in the same legislative body. Given the potential for good that might be accomplished by electing Christians to office, it may be hard for some to imagine that a down side might exist.

In the previous paragraph, I carefully avoided using the term "Christian politician," for many Christians might consider the phrase a contradiction in terms. Be that as it may, we must acknowledge that, in a democracy, policy is accomplished through compromise. Elected officials—politicians—get legislation passed by agreeing to help each other. Because it is hard to imagine that Christians would hold such a large majority in any elected body that they would be able to avoid cooperation with any non-Christian politicians, we are left with the reality that Christian politicians have to compromise to accomplish the good they seek. How can a Christian compromise when dealing with legislation he or she considers based on the principles of the gospel? Christian politicians live in a tension between the good they believe they *should* do and the good they believe they *can* do.

A second area of concern relates to the political process itself. We might focus our attention on this issue by asking the following questions: Can Christian candidates run campaigns that always, in everything, glorify God? If they cannot, do they run the risk of corrupting their faith by seeking public office? If they do run this risk, is the good they might do as elected officials worth the risk? Biblical literature repeatedly warns that those with power tend to be corrupted by power. The temptation elected officials face to use their power to further their own careers rather than the kingdom of God must be great.

Christians who do not have the desire or resources to run for office have another pathway to involvement, a pathway that has grown in popularity over the last 30 years. They may seek greater influence by forming or participating in a political movement. It is to this form of involvement that we now turn.

Political Organizing Among Christians

A Christian who equates abortion with murder joins a protest at an abortion clinic, hoping to disrupt the business conducted there on a daily basis. Another Christian who has worked serving food to the homeless at a downtown soup kitchen joins a sit-in at a run-down hotel, in which many poor residents live, in an effort to stop the owner of the building from tearing it down to make way for luxury condominiums. Both may feel they are doing the work of the kingdom of God by their direct political action. Both may feel voting or running for office are not enough to stop the spread of evil and injustice in our world. The question each must ask is whether or not Christians should be involved in this kind of political activity. Is this kind of activity an appropriate way for Christians to interact with their government? Again, we should look at the benefits and dangers of this kind of activity.

The benefits of the activity would seem obvious to the participants. They have identified an evil practice—a practice that brings harm to people who are dearly loved by God—and they are intervening to stop that practice. But what of the method? We can add a level of complexity to the issue by suggesting that at some point the owner of the abortion clinic and the owner of the building scheduled for demolition would probably get a court to issue a restraining order against the protesters. Then the actions seen as a means of promoting the values of the kingdom of God are actions ruled illegal by the government to which we are instructed to submit under normal circumstances.

A more fundamental issue has to do with the basic methods used by the protesters and other Christians in-

volved in political groups whose goals are to force change.
The Christians are involved in coercion, a practice many
would consider a veiled form of violence because it is designed to force people to behave in a certain way. As an expression of power—the protesters believe their numbers will
force people who don't want to change to change anyway—
for some Christians, this type of political activity seems to
run counter to the values embodied in the life of Jesus.

This kind of direct organization in pursuit of political
change features many of the same dangers we saw when
looking at elected officials. Christians who organize
around a cause they deeply believe in run the risk of
falling into self-righteousness—after all, they are involved
in a cause they believe *all* Christians should embrace.
They run the risk of allowing the ends to justify the means.
Historians have shown us repeated examples of Christians
working for what they believe to be a righteous cause who
have resorted to means that did not glorify God.

Conclusion

We would be hard-pressed to find a political issue
about which Christians agree. Much of the media coverage of the so-called religious right might lead the casual
observer to conclude that Christians agree much more
than they actually do. Because, as political scientists con-
firm, political beliefs are influenced by a number of factors
such as class, ethnicity, and family history, we should not
be surprised that Christians disagree. And we probably
should not seek agreement. The diverse political opinions
among Christians can be used to challenge and enrich our
beliefs. Still, we should expect at least two things from
Christians as we think about our involvement with our
government.

We should expect that we, as Christians, will be willing to treat each other with love and grace when we talk
about our various political involvements. We each walk in

the light we have at the moment. While we should remain open to illumination from the Giver of all light, we should also recognize our limits, our blind spots. In recognizing our own limitations, we can treat the limitations of others with grace. In our interaction with our government and the political world, this grace may be expressed in a number of ways. One way would be that while I honor my own political convictions, I am willing to grant that my fellow Christian's political commitments are also valid—even if they contradict my own.

And we should be willing to submit our beliefs more and more each day to the Lordship of Christ. As disciples, we should strive to submit all of what we are to the Lordship of Christ. In the traditions of many churches, this has been interpreted primarily as meaning the individual willingly submitting his or her personal habits and religious practice to Christ. Yet, surely Christ wants more than this from us. Along with our financial decisions, perhaps our political alliances—the ways we adopt to interact with our government—are the hardest to submit to the Lordship of Christ. Because it is so difficult, it is precisely what we need most to do.

Notes:

1. Nathaniel Hawthorne, *The Scarlet Letter* (New York: Penguin, 1986), 75.

2. Henry David Thoreau, "On the Duty of Civil Disobedience" (New York: New American Library, 1980), 226.

About the Author: Dr. Martin holds a Ph.D. in American Studies from the University of Minnesota. He teaches in the Department of Literature, Journalism, and Modern Languages at Point Loma Nazarene University.

At Issue: How should the Church and government live together? How should Christians react when human laws restrict our ability to follow God's law?

Common Ground: God's laws are more important than human laws.

CHAPTER 8

Government and the Church

by Cheryl Gochnauer

Without even leaving your house, you can appreciate the perks of living in a country with a strong sense of leadership. The clean water flowing from your tap; the direct line to 911 if trouble brews; the safe and constant levels of electricity powering your appliances. Each benefit, at one point or another, is regulated by a governmental agency.

Step out on the porch and check out the paved streets and emission-controlled cars. Wave as the public school bus lumbers by. Jingle the currency in your pocket. Look up as a military jet streaks across the sky. Open the mailbox and pull out your voter notification card, inviting you and others in your district to the polls to vote on local and national issues.

Of course, the government encourages our participation in other matters, too, like paying taxes, registering for the draft, and obeying the laws of the land. In fact, Washington demands our compliance for the good of the general populace.

Freedom of Religion

In the beginning, there was authority, and in every civilization since Adam and Eve left the garden, wise governing has helped create peace out of chaos. Likewise, inept or intrusive leadership has stirred unrest and undermined the confidence of those being governed.

One of the fundamental rights recognized in the United States is the ability to worship as we choose. In fact, the right of freedom of religion was so valued it was written into the Constitution in 1791, as part of that historic document's first amendment:

> Congress shall make no law respecting an establishment of religion, or prohibiting the free exercise thereof; or abridging the freedom of speech, or of the press; or the right of the people peaceably to assemble, and to petition the government for a redress of grievances.

Since many of the first immigrants headed to America to escape religious persecution in their homelands, the colonial government wanted to ensure individual beliefs would never again be dictated by the state.

Most people would agree that we don't want to create a situation where our government decides how we worship God. Yet, it's also unrealistic to think these two forces—church and state—should never interact with each other.

When church-and-state issues inevitably clash, discussion also erupts as to whether Uncle Sam should be viewed as a benevolent relative or an intimidating big brother.

In either case, the Bible is clear about where our ultimate loyalty lies. God's laws are more important than human laws, and when these two forces lock horns, our final allegiance is to Christ. At the same time, Paul admonishes us to pray for those who hold authority over us, and Jesus said to "give to Caesar what is Caesar's" (Mark 12:17).

Peter and John Before the Sanhedrin

It's not unusual for Christians to find themselves persecuted by those in power. When evil people attain key leadership positions, they can lead entire societies away from God. In the 20th century, Hitler, Stalin, and Mao inflamed their followers and encouraged the slaughter of thousands of Jews and Christians. Today, persecution continues as corrupt rulers incorporate ethnic and religious "cleansing" as part of their state objectives.

Unfortunately, a few powerful people can implement persecution, even when the general populace initially has nothing against those being targeted. This happened with Jesus, and again with His apostles.

After Pentecost, the apostles boldly proclaimed the gospel wherever they went. Peter was especially vibrant in his testimony. Thousands responded to his message and became new believers. The leading religious figures in Jerusalem, the Sanhedrin, were "greatly disturbed because the apostles were teaching the people and proclaiming in Jesus the resurrection of the dead" (Acts 4:2). So they arrested Peter and John and brought them before the Sanhedrin.

Instead of being intimidated by having to appear before the most powerful religious assembly in the land, Peter went on the offensive. When asked, in effect, who gave them the right to buck the status quo, Peter responded, "Know this, you and all the people of Israel: It is by the name of Jesus Christ of Nazareth, *whom you crucified* but whom God raised from the dead" (4:10, emphasis added). Instead of being cowed, Peter and John deflected the accusatory arrows right back at the Sanhedrin.

The religious leaders were surprised by the apostles' courage but were still determined to stop the spread of Christianity. So they commanded Peter and John not to speak or teach at all in the name of Jesus.

Yet, the apostles were resolute. "'Judge for yourselves whether it is right in God's sight to obey you rather than God,' they responded. 'For we cannot help speaking about what we have seen and heard'" (4:19-20).

The Sanhedrin threatened Peter and John some more,

then released them. Did the apostles boast to their friends about how they showed those guys who was boss? Did their followers pat them on the back and tell them how brave they were? No.

Instead, Peter and John went back to their people and told them what had happened. "When they heard this, they raised their voices together in prayer to God" (4:24). The apostles noted the evilness of the governing powers: "Indeed Herod and Pontius Pilate met together with the Gentiles and the people of Israel in this city to conspire against your holy servant Jesus, whom you anointed" (v. 27). They laid the new threats at God's feet and renewed their prayer that He would "enable your servants to speak your word with great boldness" (v. 29).

Though the Sanhedrin was corrupt, not every member favored persecuting Christians. When the apostles were once again brought before the group, Peter renewed his objection, saying, "We must obey God rather than men!" (5:29). The religious leaders were furious and wanted to put the apostles to death. However, Gamaliel, a popular Pharisee and teacher of the law, persuaded the Sanhedrin to reconsider. He suggested that if this movement were not from God, it would fail. On the other hand, if it were from God, nothing they could do would stop it. Moreover, they might find themselves fighting God himself. Ironically, that's exactly what they were doing.

Modern Religious Freedom

In more recent history, governments have continued to try to influence society through Christian values. A notable example is England's James I, who sought to put the Scriptures in the hands of the common people. So he commissioned what came to be known since 1611 as "the King James Version" of the Bible.

In America during the Civil War, the United States government began printing "In God We Trust" on two-cent coins. By 1955, legislation made the appearance of these words mandatory on all U.S. coins and paper currency. A year later, "In God We Trust" was drafted as the national motto.

Though praying in schools was outlawed by the early 1960s, at the end of the millennium chaplains for both the House of Representatives and the Senate were still beginning legislative sessions with prayer.

Although many governments still stubbornly refuse the call of Christianity, others like Russia, Albania, and Mozambique have in recent years decided to open formerly closed borders to the gospel.

Yet, are there some barriers between church and state that should remain?

Pros and Cons of the State Stepping In

At the beginning of this chapter, we read about some of the benefits citizens of the United States enjoy, including education, police and military protection, and a secure currency system. Churches usually do not pay taxes to help provide these and other services, since most income raised by religious and other nonprofit organizations is usually deemed to be tax-exempt. Likewise, religious organizations cannot expect government funding as they attempt to reach most of their evangelistic or missionary goals.

Periodically, the Pandora's box of church-state issues is opened up, and voters or judges get to cast their opinions on how much these two forces should interact. Let's examine three of the most widely debated elements:

Taxation and Licensing. There are thousands of churches in the United States. Each one represents potential tax dollars that would pour into the government's coffers, if churches were held to the same taxation standards as businesses across the land. Those tax dollars could be used to pay down the national debt or fund social services and other governmental programs that affect our neighbors and ourselves. Because the churches would be tax-payers, they would also be beneficiaries of such programs, receiving moneys themselves.

Proponents say licensing would help set standards to protect children in church-run daycare centers and schools. Periodic visits by authorities would minimize abusive situations and encourage churches to maintain healthy educational environments.

Opponents fear, however, that the state's definition of "healthy educational environment" may clash with the ideals of the church or private school board. What if the state decides that teaching a particular doctrine is divisive or damages an individual's self-esteem? The government may decide to homogenize the "offensive" teaching, limiting or prohibiting religious instruction as it already has in courthouses, city halls, and graduation auditoriums. Even on church property, it could become illegal to put up Nativity scenes or display the Ten Commandments.

"Ridiculous," say supporters. The government is not out to destroy Christianity. In fact, many Christians fancy the idea of state-funded vouchers that would allow parents to partner with the government in using educational tax dollars to send children to whatever school their parents choose, including parochial schools.

"Watch out," warn opponents. Authorities could turn off the financial tap when a church-sponsored school refuses to do things their way. That picture of Jesus in the office? Forget it. The state is sure to ban any overtly religious symbols.

Employment Laws. Shouldn't an owner have free rein in hiring whomever he or she feels is best suited to a particular position? In the secular world, the answer is maybe. Yes, owners can hire whomever they want, as long as they've been fair in considering all available candidates. Discrimination laws prohibit business owners from bypassing any qualified applicant solely on the basis of race, sex, or religion.

At face value, letting everyone have a crack at a certain job seems the right thing to do. Fair is fair. Those who propose holding churches to the same employment law requirements as the rest of the land want to protect the rights of all individuals. Why shouldn't every man and woman be guaranteed the right to apply and be considered for any position they desire?

Opponents assert that what's fair for the individual may not be fair for the employer. While a person's race should never be used to exclude him or her from consideration, in some cases, the employer may decide to pass on a potential applicant specifically because of his or her religion or sexual orientation. Because the beliefs of some applicants are in total conflict with those of the employer, all parties can end up in a no-win situation. For instance, how can a church that teaches that practicing homosexuality is a sin hire an openly gay person? Should a deli be required to recruit, and then make special provisions for, an employee who refuses to handle certain meats because of his or her religious beliefs?

Should an evangelistic Christian have the same freedom of expression rights on the job as an outspoken atheist? It seems intrinsically discriminatory to ban religious tracts in the same shop that allows pornographic posters on lockers. However, maybe it's best to live a silent witness, without all the flash of opened Bibles and WWJD jewelry.

Perhaps.

But remember, when Christ instructed us to "go and make disciples of all nations . . . teaching them to obey everything I have commanded you" (Matthew 28:19-20), He didn't add, "except between 9 and 5." Each individual will have to decide how to fulfill the Great Commission as he or she ministers within his or her workplace, either as an employee or an employer.

Taking Care of the Poor. Although retirement benefits and welfare are considered automatic entitlements by many, these programs have only been in the United States since the 1930s. Before President Roosevelt signed them into existence, relatives usually banded together to take care of their own. However, the Great Depression devastated the country, and it was necessary for the government to step in as entire families lost their jobs and their homes.

Looking back to the first century A.D., Acts 4:32-35 describes the way the early believers watched out for each other: "No one claimed that any of his possessions was his own, but they shared everything they had. . . . There were no needy persons among them."

Now that the Great Depression is over and the United States is enjoying its strongest economy ever, would our present government still need to provide retirement and welfare systems if the church was following the example set by Christians 2,000 years ago?

It is commonly said that 10 percent of church members carry the load for the other 90 percent. This applies in teaching, volunteering, and in making financial contributions. What a ministry the church would have if all the members obeyed God's command to "bring the whole tithe into the storehouse" (Malachi 3:10)! The congregation could take care of its own needy members and still have plenty to share with the surrounding community.

Nevertheless, until the other 90 percent of church members step forward and accept God's mandate, the government will have to bear most of the burden of taking care of the poor, with charitable organizations, individual churches, and religious groups supplementing their work.

A Word Aptly Spoken

When we find ourselves in the midst of clashing church-and-state issues, it's important to follow Jesus' assertion to "be as shrewd as snakes and as innocent as doves" (Matthew 10:16). Since leaders hold only the power God allows them, we need to maintain as much harmony as possible between the two factions. That way, each side can better achieve their God-ordained goals.

However, if conflict escalates to a point where we have to choose between obeying our government or obeying God, we need to follow the apostles' example: "We must obey God rather than men."

Once that ardent stand is taken, be confident. "The Lord is near. Do not be anxious about anything, but in everything, by prayer and petition, with thanksgiving, present your requests to God. And the peace of God, which transcends all understanding, will guard your hearts and your minds in Christ Jesus" (Philippians 4:5-7).

Background Scripture: Matthew 10:16; 28:19-20; Mark 12:17; Acts 4:1-35; 5:29; Philippians 4:6-7

About the Author: Cheryl Gochnauer is a freelance writer who lives in Kansas City. She is the author of *So You Want to Be a Stay-at-home Mom.*

At Issue: *Where should or do our children receive their moral education? What happens when the government takes over education and does not teach morality? Who should pay for education—public taxes or private funds?*

Common Ground: *Children should be taught the ways of the Lord.*

CHAPTER 9

Education

by Cheryl Gochnauer

Two, four, six, eight. Who do we appreciate?" When it comes to the classroom, some disillusioned parents mutter, "Everyone but Christ."

I can understand their reaction. My daughter Karen's first foray into our local public school system lasted exactly three weeks. I'm all for learning our sounds and letters, but in less than a month, my fresh-faced kindergartner managed to acquire a vocabulary that made Terry, my truck-driver husband, blush—and he's heard it all.

Terry and I are well aware that the primary responsibility for raising our kids falls squarely on our shoulders. Deuteronomy 6:6-7 is clear: "These commandments that I give you today are to be upon your hearts. Impress them on your children. Talk about them when you sit at home and when you walk along the road, when you lie down and when you get up." Proverbs 22:6 is just as succinct: "Train a child in the way he should go, and when he is old he will not turn from it."

We get the point and gladly accept the assignment. Yet, is it too much for us to ask for a little backup from the other teachers in our children's lives?

Since I couldn't attend classes with Karen—for one thing, I'd look ridiculous squeezed into one of those pint-sized chairs—I expected the teacher to act as my on-the-spot advocate. Unfortunately, in this case, my trust was misplaced. Freedom of expression ranked higher in this particular classroom than cultivating clean speech. Motherly indignation flamed. "She's OUTTA there!"

The search for an alternative was on.

Public Schools—a Basic Primer

Public schools haven't always run the risk of being considered humanistic hothouses. There was a time when cursing and related misbehavior automatically translated into swift and certain punishment: a missed activity, a trip to the principal's office, a suspension. America's earliest schools, established by Puritans flooding into the "new" land in the 1600s, reflected the majority belief that the "Rs" of education—"Reading, 'Rriting, and 'Rithmetic"— were not complete without "Religion."

Jewish families in America have long recognized the importance of a strong partnership between religious and basic scholastic education. For them, passing on ancient Hebrew tradition is a nonnegotiable facet. Day schools (full-time Jewish schools), afternoon Hebrew schools (a few hours a week, in addition to public schooling), and Sunday morning religious training all are used to infuse Jewish boys and girls with an appreciation of their heritage.

For several hundred years, God's place in the classroom was ensured. However, in the 20th century, a discernible shift in values began building momentum. Strident voices convinced lawmakers that instructing children about Christ was tantamount to shackling them with government-decreed religion.

Before the century was half over, the U.S. Supreme Court decided that public schools would be off-limits for compulsory religious education (1948). Within another 15 years, even school prayer was banned.

Teachers are forbidden to share their faith. Nowhere is this more evident than in the current debates about evolution and creationism. Individual students invite disciplinary action or disdain for wearing religious clothing or jewelry. The Ten Commandments have been removed; "anything goes" philosophies have taken their place.

Public Accusations and Defenses

Alas, morality in the schoolhouse is dead. Or is it? I thought so, as I swiftly snatched kindergartner Karen from her less-than-nurturing atmosphere.

Yet, just as our nation is made up of many different states, our school systems are comprised of a mixture of various administrators and teachers. Even within the same district, parents can point out the "good" schools and the "bad" ones. Government regulations aside, authority figures in individual schools are the ones who set the tone for what transpires there.

Look how much impact a dozen committed men—the apostles—had on the world. Within a secular school setting, many parents, as well as their children, also welcome the opportunity to be salt and light.

It is not necessary to wear a badge that screams our Christian status in order to affect positive change. Even Jesus never walked up to a group of people, stuck out His hand, and introduced himself as "Jesus, Son of God. And you are . . . ?" Instead, He simply loved. In action and in deed, He taught people how to live moral lives.

Likewise, Christians, positioned to act, can and do quietly influence school policy. Elaine Swanigan, a Kansas City mom who has a child in a suburban high school, another in junior high, and a third in kindergarten, was inspired by the words of a pastor friend. "He said one of the most influential positions someone can have is to be on the school board, because they make decisions about curriculum. They set the tone for everything."

There's no doubt there are perks associated with attending public school too. Number one, parents don't have to make tuition payments. Bus transportation is usually provided. Extracurricular activities like sports or cheerleading, band and choir, science and art fairs, and a variety of intramural competitions are readily available in most schools. College preparatory classes pave the way to higher education at secular colleges and universities, with the promise of government-sponsored scholarships to those who achieve high marks.

Surrounding homes funnel kids into the neighborhood school, and those same kids play together in their backyards after classes. For those who view public schools as a mission field, this proximity provides continuous chances to share the gospel. Friendships started in the classroom can translate into witnessing opportunities while working together on homework or shooting hoops after school.

"What would happen if every Christian pulled out of public school? I'm talking students, teachers, and administration. That's scary to me," Elaine muses.

For other parents, especially those of elementary students, it can be discomforting to send their little lambs among perceived wolves. These moms and dads doubt if their children will be strong enough to pick up a stone to defeat the in-your-face Goliaths. So they seek other options.

A Private Matter

As I signed the check to enroll Karen in a private Christian school, I sighed. The pricey tuition tightened our already stretched budget; no more "mad money" around our house. But I also felt relieved. Here, my daughter would have our family's moral and religious values reinforced everyday. I could look forward to more verses than curses escaping her little lips.

So it was. The transformation was remarkable—and a little sobering. I realized my daughter, at least at this stage of her young life, was highly susceptible to the influences around her. Fortunately, one of those influences was a tenderhearted teacher who led Karen and several of her classmates to the Lord one April afternoon.

When these youngsters began asking questions about God, there was no need for furtive glances at the hallway door, wondering if the conversation was being overheard. There also were no patronizing comments, assigning Christ status a little lower than Santa Claus and the Easter Bunny.

Instead, the private school teacher was able to follow where her discerning spirit led. Questions were asked and answered. Heads were bowed, and schoolchildren prayed. After my daughter's conversion, I watched Karen begin a relationship with God, increasingly anchored by her own personal experiences with Him.

Jesus values childlike trust. In fact, He said that without it, no one can enter the kingdom of heaven (Matthew 18:3). Whatever educational path we choose for our kids, parents have a special responsibility to guard that trust and preserve it.

Some parents consider Christian schools to be spiritual greenhouses. Young, impressionable kids are nurtured within a controlled environment. Then, when their roots are deep and they're strong enough, they're transplanted into the secular world.

Others fear their youngsters will become too sheltered and end up alienated from their peers in secular schools. They wonder how a "naive" kid can make it in today's society.

In parochial classrooms, subjects from astronomy to zoology are interpreted through a Christian worldview. It would be foolish to assume that private school protects our children from all secular influences. Drugs and alcohol, improper sexual conduct, and jaded attitudes, while less common than in public schools, still manage to seep into even the best religious academies.

Still, these negative influences are less prevalent within the walls of a private school. One common thread unites each student: Behind every child there is at least one parent or guardian who is committed to raising that child in the "nurture and admonition of the Lord" (Ephesians 6:4, KJV).

These parents have decided that when conflicts arise, their children will know how to solve problems from a Christian perspective. When hormones start raging, there's a greater chance the young man or woman sitting next to their daughter or son will also share the moral values the parents have stressed at home.

Private school kids are buffered, with Mom and Dad on one side and educators on the other.

No Place Like Home

Kindergarten passed; then first grade, and second. Karen was thriving, but our budget was going down for the third time, gasping whenever I wrote that monthly check to pay for her private schooling. Also, I was straining against the confines of a full-time job that neutralized the amount of time I had each day with my daughter.

Why can't my representatives get moving on these school voucher programs? I fretted. I want to have a choice, to use those tax dollars to educate Karen where I want to, not where the state decrees. Nevertheless, debates over vouchers bogged down in the legislature. Uncle Sam would be no help, at least at this time.

Terry and I had to choose which would be more beneficial to Karen: enjoying full-time Christian schooling but having very little face-to-face interaction with Mom, or chucking the tuition payment and bringing Karen home with me. We decided I would quit my job, become a stay-at-home mom, and home-school our little girl.

Christians seeking to incorporate their faith with their curriculum comprise the bulk of home schoolers. However, there are also thousands of secular-minded parents who are now considering the benefits of individualized study. As classrooms continue to expand with increasingly unbalanced teacher/student ratios and scholastic achievement rates decline, more families are taking back the educational reins.

Home schoolers believe there's no one better suited to train up their children, no matter what the subject, than the parents. The one-on-one instruction and flexibility to adjust curriculum to conform to the student's individual strengths and weaknesses makes home schooling an attractive choice.

Is your daughter exhibiting a talent for mathematics? You can zero in on this skill, meeting the challenge of the student who is no longer cooling her heels while the rest of the class catches up. Is your son having trouble with language arts? If he's home-schooled, you can nurture him in this problem area until light dawns.

Socialization usually arises as the primary argument against home schooling:

"Won't he become isolated, sheltered in an unrealistic bubble that skews his worldview?"

"How will she learn to interact with other children if you take her out of school?"

Many parents believe that home schooling actually enhances their child's social skills. By pulling their child out of the traditional classroom and getting him or her off the public school playgrounds, peer pressure is minimized, effectively neutralizing the primary threat to his or her self-esteem.

What about participating in sports? Spelling bees? Music competitions? Restrictions vary from state to state, but the law sometimes requires local school districts to allow home schoolers access to extracurricular activities. Private schools often welcome home schoolers to enroll in special classes, like computer and band, which require special equipment or a group setting. Also, home-schooling families sometimes link up, with one mother teaching language and social studies, for example, while the other mom teaches math and science.

Home-schooled children are encouraged to think out-side the box. No longer is education hemmed in by age, location, or the dictates of the local school board. Reli-gious beliefs are freely incorporated into the day's lesson. Instead of just reading about politics, families can jump in the car and head for the capitol. No need to wait for a planned field trip or school holiday; their classroom trav-els with them.

Academic standards are just as stringent as in any other educational setting; there are minimal goals to be met. In fact, most states require keeping a log to insure students are being adequately educated. Still, the teaching and testing to achieve those goals can take place any time of day, any day of the week.

A Complete Circle

After linking up with a local home-schooling support group and pouring over catalogs, Terry and I selected cur-riculum and prepared to start home-schooling Karen in the fall. A few weeks before school started, a friend from church, Robin, called. Her daughter Tiffany was the same age as Karen and was one of her best friends. "I've been thinking about your reasons for wanting to home-school—the finances and your bad experience with the local school. But I wanted to let you know that things there have changed.

"The new principal's a Christian. Many of the teach-ers on staff are believers," Robin continued. She had been selected as the head room-mother over the third-grade classes and would be able to influence activities chosen. "We can request one of the Christian teachers, and ask the school to place Karen and Tiffany in the same class-room, so they'll each have a Christian friend right there."

A God-fearing principal, teacher, room-mother, and classmate. "You'll never find a better situation in public school than this," Robin said. "Why don't you give it a try?"

I contacted the school and made an appointment to visit with the principal. Walking through the silent halls together, I expressed my concerns, and he sought to assure me. Shaking his hand, I headed home with hope in my heart.

Could it work? Terry and I decided to take a chance. I placed Karen's home-schooling curriculum on a shelf in my closet, where I could grab it in an instant, if need be.

Entering the same doors we'd exited three years before, we enrolled Karen in public school. I could see the red brick building from my back porch and kept a vigilant watch over my little one, pouring over her backpack and monitoring her classroom. This time, she was stronger. Crude language didn't follow her home. The three years of Christian school training and having Christ in her heart fortified her. Third grade flew by, then fourth, and fifth.

Karen is now in sixth grade, at the same public school. We take it a year at a time, always ready to make a change, if necessary. But so far, so good.

What's the right choice for your own children—public, private, or home schooling? No matter which arena you choose, active parental involvement is crucial. God is intimately interested in where we educate our children. It's important to keep Him at the center of our decisions. Listen to His still, small voice, and choose the educational route that best fits your individual child.

Background Scripture: Deuteronomy 6:6-7; Proverbs 22:6; Matthew 18:3; Acts 17:26; Ephesians 6:4

About the Author: Cheryl Gochnauer is a freelance writer who lives in Kansas City. Cheryl speaks to women's groups and ministers to parents through her web site.

At Issue: *How can we show love to persons without condoning their sin? Or how can we proclaim God's grace to sinners and be faithful to proclaim God's judgment on sin?*

Common Ground: *Christians have been redeemed by God's grace, and we have a responsibility to proclaim the Good News to others.*

CHAPTER 10

Sin and Sinner

by Gaymon Bennett

Herman Melville, assessing the fiction of his friend and fellow author Nathaniel Hawthorne, wrote: it "derives its force from its appeal to that . . . sense of Innate Depravity and Original Sin, from whose visitations, in some shape or other, no deeply thinking mind is always and wholly free."[1] Melville, a secular writer, needed no more evidence for the reality of sin than observable human behavior. Christians, however, like to be able to point to the Bible— to chapter and verse—to define and prove their beliefs.

But, while the Bible discusses the problem of sin, it assumes sin's reality without much definition or proof. The Bible does make clear that sin is destructive and ultimately deadly—a plight from which sinners cannot save themselves. It is indeed such a serious problem that God sent His Son to earth with the instructions that He was to be called "Jesus, because he will save his people from their sins" (Matthew 1:21). When Jesus dined with His newly called disciple Matthew, and the Pharisees asked why He ate with tax collectors and sinners, Jesus replied, "I have not come to call the righteous, but sinners" (Matthew 9:13; Mark 2:7; and Luke 5:32).

Taking Sin Seriously

Taking Christianity seriously, therefore, requires taking sin seriously. Richard Taylor in *A Right Conception of Sin* calls sin the "common denominator of the other doctrines"[2] of Christianity. And John Wesley goes so far as to state, "If, therefore we take away this foundation, that man is by nature foolish and sinful . . . the Christian system falls apart at once."[3]

Christians agree on the following core doctrines:

- Sin is real and is a real problem.
- Sin has corrupted human nature.
- Sin is a condition of the heart.
- Sin manifests itself in broken relationships.
- Subtle sins of the spirit are as destructive as gross sins of the flesh.
- Sin cannot be remedied by human action.
- God loves, seeks, and wants to redeem sinners.
- Christians are responsible to reach out in love to sinners.

Whether we define sin, as John Wesley did, as a "voluntary transgression of a known law"[4] of God, more broadly as an act or attitude contrary to and falling short of God's standard for us, or—as some recent writers contend—as any act of violence against God's creation, Christians agree that sin is real, and a real problem. They also agree that the Fall, however understood, has distorted the image of God in us, and that we have strayed a long way from our created goodness. Sin has corrupted our very natures.

Sin Begins in the Heart

Although many Christians identify certain acts as sinful, all recognize that sin begins in the heart. Jesus said in the Sermon on the Mount, "You have heard that . . . 'anyone who murders will be subject to judgment.' But I tell you that anyone who is angry with his brother will be subject to judgment" (Matthew 5:21-22). It follows that sin is, or manifests itself in, broken relationships. It sets us at odds with God, with others, and even with ourselves.

God is the source of our spiritual lives, and fellowship with Him is what we were created for. No wonder the apostle Paul described the disobedient Ephesians as "dead in your transgressions and sins" (Ephesians 2:1). Sin separates a sinner not only from God but also from fellow humans. Acknowledged sin, such as adultery, can tear a family apart, but unacknowledged sin, such as envy and spite, can also destroy relationships. Envy and spite are not just hurtful to others but are damaging to one's self and—if not remedied—damning to one's soul. That suggests that sin need not be gross or criminal in its consequences to be destructive. All Christians understand that as horrible as the sins of the flesh may be, sins of the spirit are also damaging, though we often tend to be more forgiving of them.

How can we become the persons we were intended to be, the persons Jesus modeled for us in His life on earth? Christians regard our sin-debt as beyond our ability to pay, or our sin-sickness as beyond our own remedy. Neither good intentions nor good works, neither penance nor piety alone can free and heal sinners from their sins. True repentance is required, of course, but would be ineffectual without the atoning sacrifice of Jesus Christ. God in love seeks to forgive and restore sinners, and to renew the image of God in them. Heaven rejoices when even one sinner repents.

Reaching Out

Finally, Christians agree that, as forgiven sinners, we should reach out in love to those who need forgiveness. Though the apostle Paul suggested that unrepentant sin warrants judgment and even expulsion from the church (1 Corinthians 5:13), the Bible instructs us to turn sinners from their errors to save them from death (James 5:20), even to forgive, comfort, and love those who have sinned and caused us grief (2 Corinthians 2:7). In His life, Jesus demonstrated the proper attitude toward sinners, and J. Wilbur Chapman's hymn "Our Great Savior" captures it in these words:

Jesus! What a Friend for sinners! . . .
He, my Savior, makes me whole.[5]

Christians can agree on these core doctrines and still disagree on the interpretation and application of them; they can agree in principle about how to treat the sinner and still differ in practice. Christians can, for example, hold differing beliefs about how grace operates on the sinner. Some of these beliefs have affected Holiness theology through the medium of American popular religious culture. Among these is the belief that Jesus Christ's atoning blood *covers* sin without necessarily changing the sinner's nature. For years, Holiness congregations have sung the refrain: "My sins are all covered by the blood." A result of this belief is the idea that, though forgiven, Christians may continue sinning. Others, however, believe that the atoning blood can, as another gospel song states, "wash away sin"—that is, cleanse the sinner and transform the sinful nature. Atoning grace not only forgives the *sin* but empowers the Christian to live in holiness.

These differences affect the way Christians and churches treat sinners. Those who believe the former are more optimistic about God's grace for forgiveness than for transformation. They tend to emphasize witnessing to sinners and the act of conversion. Those who believe the latter tend to emphasize the process of Christian growth in grace and are more optimistic about God's grace for transformation. Thankfully, many churches emphasize God's abundant grace for both forgiveness and transformation.

Sharing Abundant Grace

How can we Christians present this abundant grace to those who need it? The "what would Jesus do?" question has become a cliché, and as a bumper sticker, it is "pearls before pigs" (Matthew 7:6). However, for the Christian seeking guidance, it is the right place to begin.

Jesus shocked the established church of His day by

sharing table fellowship with sinners. He invited himself to the home of Zacchaeus, the wealthy tax collector, inviting loud criticism because He was the "guest of a 'sinner'" (Luke 19:7). The story implies that without any prompting other than being in the presence of Jesus, Zacchaeus repented of his sin and promised to make restitution.

On several occasions Jesus offered forgiveness for those caught in the act of sinning. Once when the Pharisees brought a woman caught in adultery to Jesus, He challenged anyone without sin to throw the first stone at her. When everyone skulked away, Jesus asked the woman who was left to condemn her.

She answered, "No one, sir."

Jesus said, "Then neither do I condemn you. . . . Go and leave your life of sin" (John 8:11).

Another time when He was the guest of Simon the Pharisee, and a sinful but contrite woman bowed before Jesus, bathed His feet with her tears, wiped them with her hair, kissed them, and perfumed them. When His host complained, Jesus responded with a brief parable and a sharp rebuke. Then He forgave the woman's sins (see Luke 7:36-50). Jesus' compassion toward sinners, such as this woman, contrasts sharply with His harsh words for most of the religious folk of His day. He made it clear that their self-righteousness was worse than the sins of the repentant.

Sin and Sinner

Jesus was uncompromising about sin. He didn't ignore it; He forgave it. His attitude is represented in the expression, "Hate the sin; love the sinner," a sentiment most of us agree with whether we succeed in putting it into practice or not. Consider the following possibilities for separating the sin from the sinner in order to deal with *persons*.

Christians can put this principle into practice by befriending coworkers or neighbors, planning activities together, and seeking opportunities to talk about spiritual matters. Many churches provide Sunday School classes or seminars in "friendship evangelism." Churches can also help their members by providing attractive "seeker friendly" programs that they can invite their non-Christian friends to attend. Increasingly churches are providing more diverse ministries to reach and meet the needs of their constituents including the unchurched or "prechurched" (as they are sometimes identified). These ministries often include support groups for recovering addicts and recently divorced individuals. Most of us have known (and some of us have been) sinners drawn by the Holy Spirit and the invitation of friends into Christian fellowship.

Even though such programs and ministries do draw sinners into the church, they may not accomplish the goal of helping us separate the sin from the sinner. Doing so is difficult for a variety of psychological and social reasons. Consider these two:

The first has to do with the motives of Christians and the suspicions of sinners. Even if we are sincere in our desire to love sinners, if our ulterior motive is to change them, we shouldn't be surprised if they are suspicious of our efforts. Expecting to enjoy concerts, mother-daughter teas, or sports activities, then being confronted with the gospel message, our unsaved friends may recoil, feel condemned, or actually be driven away.

The second difficulty has to do with the dynamics of an established Christian fellowship and the suspicions of its members. Individuals joining any group feel—for a while, at least—like outsiders. Add to that feelings of inadequacy or guilt and assumptions about church or Christianity, and they will be even more uncomfortable. Some members of the fellowship will appear to be indifferent and some will be suspicious.

Regarding the first difficulty, it is probably better to be forthright when inviting non-Christian friends to outreach programs even if that risks temporary rejection. Permanent rejection is unlikely if we are truly friends and not merely salvation salespersons. God will prepare the hearts of the friends we want to bring to Christ (John 12:32). I have observed my father on several occasions speak forthrightly to non-Christians about their need for Christ, and almost without fail they have responded contritely and gratefully because his concern was clearly motivated by love.

Regarding the second difficulty, I believe that most Christians welcome sinners, want to draw them into Christian fellowship, and minister God's grace to them. But I also believe that most of us don't do that very well. Evangelism methods and outreach programs are useful but limited in their effectiveness unless—as in Zacchaeus' house—the presence of Jesus is at the center.

Down to Specifics

To get down to specifics, how do we (and how should we) treat sinners (or those considered, at least by some, to be sinners) in the church?

There was a time, not too long ago, when divorce was not countenanced in any church. Some still consider divorce as an unpardonable sin; however, as divorce has become more common among Christians, those attitudes have changed. But questions remain in many Christians' minds. Should divorced persons serve on church boards, hold church offices, or be in positions of leadership? If not, why not; and to what purpose? How can churches be most redemptive?

Like divorce, such sexual practices as fornication, adultery, and homosexuality may be condoned by law but are condemned by the church. In recent years many Christians and some churches have singled out homosexuals and condemned homosexuality. A few Christian extremists have called AIDS God's vengeance on homosexuals. Though some churches have provided fellowships for gays and lesbians, questions about homosexuality abound. Why do some Christians seem rather indifferent to heterosexual sin while crusading against homosexuals? Isn't adultery, which fractures families and harms children, at least an equal evil? Should Holiness churches do more to present the gospel to homosexuals?

Many churches provide ministries in prisons, but few released prisoners are taken into the fellowship of those churches when they get out. On the few occasions when former felons do join Christian fellowships, they are invariably viewed by some with suspicion. What can the church do to translate its reports of prison conversions into the success of maturing Christians supported by a nurturing fellowship? Must church members be suspicious or fearful? Can individuals change? How optimistic are we about God's transforming and sanctifying grace?

Conclusion

In summary, the Bible as well as our experience confirms that "all have sinned and fall short of the glory of God, *and* are justified freely by his grace through the redemption that came by Christ Jesus" (Romans 3:23-24, emphasis added). Having received God's grace, how can we best minister it to others? Though sinners are under God's judgment, *we* need not judge them (Luke 6:37). In fact the miracle of God's grace in our own lives should enlarge our mercy toward others. It is, therefore, the grace of God and the joy of the experience of Christ that we should proclaim.

The means to this end is love. As difficult as it may be, we must love sinners as God loves them. Though we do not condone their sins, our love should not be conditioned upon their forsaking their sins. Indeed, John Wesley insisted, "Love your neighbor, not only your friend, your family that loves you . . . but a neighbor that you know is sinful and unthankful . . . That one, love as yourself . . . with the same invariable thirst for that person's hope."[6] When we do reach out in love, God will make opportunities for us to speak to the unconverted evangelistically—if we are ready.

John Fischer, a popular Christian speaker, tells the story of a young Christian who wore a "witnessing T-shirt," anticipating that someone would ask him about it, and the question would give him opportunity to share his faith. After several weeks of not being asked, the young man stopped wearing the shirt. A few days later he fell into conversation with another young man with whom he seemed to have a lot in common. Before long their conversation turned to spiritual topics, and the young Christian led his new friend into a relationship with Christ.

"By the way," the young Christian asked, "why did you stop and talk with me?"

"It was the Fender guitar T-shirt you were wearing," he said. "I play guitar, and you looked like the kind of guy I'd like to talk to."

It is a matter of being available, so that when people become aware of Jesus in our lives, we can "give them an answer" when they ask about "the reason for the hope" we have (1 Peter 3:15).

Notes:

1. By a Virginian Spending July in Vermont (pseudonym), "Hawthorne and His Mosses," *Literary World*, August 17 and August 25, 1850, n.p.

2. Richard S. Taylor, *A Right Conception of Sin* (Kansas City: Nazarene Publishing House, 1939), 9.

3. John Wesley, "The Doctrine of Original Sin" in *The Works of John Wesley* (Kansas City: Beacon Hill Press of Kansas City, 1986), 9:194.

4. John Wesley, *A Plain Account of Christian Perfection* (Kansas City: Beacon Hill Press of Kansas City, 1966), 54.

5. J. Wilbur Chapman, "Our Great Savior," *Sing to the Lord* (Kansas City: Lillenas Publishing Co., 1993), 109.

6. John Wesley, "The Way to the Kingdom" in *The Works of John Wesley* (Kansas City: Beacon Hill Press of Kansas City, 1986), 5:79.

Background Scripture: Matthew 1:21; 5:21-22; 7:6; 9:13; Mark 2:7; Luke 5:32; 6:37; 8:36-50; 19:7; John 8:11; 21:32;

Romans 3:23; 1 Corinthians 5:15; 2 Corinthians 5:7;
Ephesians 2:1; James 5:20; 1 Peter 3:15

About the Author: Dr. Gaymon Bennett is chair of the English
department at Northwest Nazarene University, Nampa, Idaho.

At Issue: Do certain criminals deserve to die? Is it better to lock them up for life or to put them to death? Do Christians have a responsibility to help apply God's justice?

Common Ground: All human life is valuable.

CHAPTER 11

Capital Punishment

by Gene Van Note

Did you ever do anything really dumb?

I have.

When I was a naive young pastor, I succumbed to the pitch of a "snake oil" salesman. Actually, he wasn't selling a magic elixir off the back of a horse-drawn wagon, but something "better." He offered me the once-in-a-lifetime opportunity to help the children in our church see the deathly sorrow a life of crime could bring.

Deathly sorrow?

Absolutely. He was touring the country, supporting himself by displaying an electric chair, one he claimed had seen years of service at Sing Sing Prison in New York State. He said he had obtained the chair because a new and improved model had been developed. I never thought to ask him how he came into possession of the Sing Sing chair or if, in fact, it was the real thing. He offered "shock treatment" against the evils of crime, if you please. He assured me that once children heard his presentation they would always live good, upstanding lives, abhorring life's darker side.

On reflection, I wonder how I could have done something so irresponsible. I was young, and he was an excellent salesman. Seventy children and a number of adults gave him their undivided attention as he spoke. Every time he placed his hand on the chair, the children sat straight up, as if they had been hit with an electric jolt.

Moments after he started, I wanted to throw him and his chair out the back door and hide my head in shame.

That experience taught me that I needed to be far more careful who I allowed to speak to our children, and that people have a morbid fascination with death. I also learned that the more you talk about something, the less important it becomes. It's like the boy crying, "Wolf," in Aesop's Fable. The electric chair man touched the lethal furniture so often while he talked that soon the crowd lost interest in it. By the time he wanted them to focus their attention on the instrument of officially sanctioned death, they were looking out the window.

Something like that is happening with regard to capital punishment. The leaders holler, and the people look out the window. In the clatter and din, life-and-death issues lose their significance—unless they're *my* life or *my* death or that of someone I admire, love, or hate. Either that, or I've made up my mind on state-sponsored executions and don't want to consider any alternative to my personal view.

A Moment's Reflection

"I wouldn't go back to my teen years, even if I could."

"Why not?"

"That was the most difficult time of my life. All I had was problems and no answers."

Most adults agree with the opinion expressed by this 38-year-old mother of two. Adulthood has its problems. Some of them are far more severe than anything faced in the teen years. Yet, one of the benefits of adulthood is that we have "thought through," or at least survived, many of life's challenges. That's one reason why adults have fewer crises than teens do. Likely it's the reason why older people seem tranquil in spite of some really tough problems. They've heard the expression, "Don't sweat the small stuff." And they don't.

Still, having stubbornly made up our minds on issues can lead to hardening of the brain, dimming of the eyes, and callouses on the eardrums, blocking any new idea that challenges the conclusions with which we are comfortable. "Children listen and read to learn; adults [do so] to find arguments to support their prejudgments," says one expert.

However, when I corral my wandering thoughts, I am confronted with the reality that Christians, unless they have totally lost their voices, have something vital to say about the seemingly endless line of people on death row.

The Capital Punishment Debate

After a varied history of support for capital punishment, the U.S. Supreme Court ruled in 1972 that the laws then on the books authorizing the death penalty amounted to cruel and unusual punishment and, therefore, were unconstitutional. So state legislatures changed the criminal codes and in 1976 the Supreme Court gave constitutional approval to the new laws and capital punishment once again became legal. Since that time, the states have executed more than 600 people. The current death-row population in the United States is estimated to be about 3,500.

Yet, the controversy continues. No other nation in the world is caught in the throes of a debate over capital punishment as is the United States. In the United States two out of every three adults support the death penalty, if the opinion polls are correct. Nevertheless, the national fabric is torn apart over this issue.

Karla Faye Tucker has become a "poster child" of the intensity and complexity of the debate. In the early 1980s she participated in the brutal murder of two people in Houston, Texas. She admitted her role in the murders and that she was a drug addict who was using several different drugs at the time of the killings. Fifteen years later, she was still an inmate of Texas's death row.

Routinely, death-row prisoners are held in their cells for 23 hours a day. It is not unusual for them to turn to education and/or religion while awaiting their fate. Some have earned college degrees. Karla Tucker turned to religion and testified that she had become a born-again Christian.

Capital punishment activists on both sides of the issue were placed in unusual positions by her clear testimony of Christian conversion. Even some "hard on crime" preachers urged the governor of Texas to commute her death penalty to life imprisonment without parole because of her rehabilitation.

Family members lined up on different sides. The brother of one of the victims campaigned for the death sentence to be commuted while that victim's husband cried out for Tucker to be executed. The governor of Texas chose not to intervene, and Karla Faye Tucker was executed in February 1998, the first woman to be executed in Texas in 120 years.

The Controversy Continues

Christians agree that murder is a serious crime and the perpetrator should be punished. All accept as fact that an executed murderer will never murder again. Who would disagree with that?

At that point Christians take different paths. Some insist that there is ample biblical evidence that a person who commits a capital crime has forfeited the right to live. They point to numerous Old Testament examples. They suggest that, if you don't want to be executed, don't commit a capital crime. Other Christians, using especially the New Testament, reach different conclusions. They sometimes point out the example of Jesus, who stopped the execution of the woman who had been caught committing adultery (John 8:1-11). Perhaps we would all benefit if we stepped back from the controversy long enough to listen to one another talk about capital punishment. To tune our ears to what others are saying, without, at the same time, piling up our arguments to destroy their position on this serious issue.

To help us listen and learn, here are some of the key arguments for and against capital punishment.

Arguments for Capital Punishment

Persons found guilty by the court of crimes that are punishable by death should be executed for these reasons:

- The Bible calls for the death penalty for murderers (Exodus 21:23-25 and similar scriptures).
- It is the only punishment that adequately expresses society's abhorrence of certain heinous crimes.
- Society has the right and obligation to protect itself from violent people. It is not the fault of good, law-abiding citizens if a person commits a heinous crime. People must be held accountable for their actions. Execution is a self-inflicted wound.
- Capital punishment is a deterrent. Statistics don't always reveal this because some things cannot be measured. We don't know how many people choose not to commit a capital crime because they know that, if caught, they will be executed.

Steven D. Stewart, prosecuting attorney of Clark County, Indiana, said recently, "Along with two-thirds of the public, I believe in capital punishment. I believe that there are some defendants who have earned the ultimate punishment our society has to offer by committing murder with aggravating circumstances present. I believe life is sacred. It cheapens the life of an innocent murder victim to say that society has no right to keep the murderer from ever killing again. In my view, society has not only the right, but the duty to act in self defense to protect the innocent. . . . Life without parole does not eliminate the risk that the prisoner will murder a guard or another inmate, and we should not be compelled to take that risk."[1]

Arguments Against Capital Punishment

The United States should abolish the practice of executing persons convicted of capital crime because:

- There is no clear New Testament teaching calling for the execution of criminals. Jesus taught that we should love people rather than hate or destroy them.
- Murder is wrong whether committed by an individual or by the state. It has a brutalizing, hardening impact on people, reducing their appreciation of the sacredness of life. For 120 years no woman was executed in Texas, but after Carla Faye Tucker's execution another woman was executed in Texas a month later.
- Capital punishment has not been shown to be a deterrent in most cases.
- Capital punishment is unfairly administered. The poor and minorities are more often executed than the rich and famous. So-called swift justice can result in the execution of innocent people, especially if they have few financial resources.
- As Christians, our natural desire for justice must be tempered with mercy.

Retired Supreme Court Justice William J. Brennan said in 1996, "The barbaric death penalty violates our Constitution. Even the most vile murderer does not release the state from its obligation to respect dignity, for the state does not honor the victim by emulating his murderer. Capital punishment's fatal flaw is that it treats people as objects to be toyed with and discarded. . . . One day the Court will outlaw the death penalty. Permanently."[2]

Where Does That Leave Us?

Given the inflamed emotions in the current debate over the death penalty, every person who is walked from his or her cell to the death chamber is given "15 minutes of fame." Television crews with blazing lights record candlelight vigils against a background of rock walls and razor wire. At the same time others rejoice that they finally have "closure" on a dark chapter of their life.

Only an extremely small minority of us knows or even imagines that we would ever know anyone living on death row or dying at the hand of an executioner. Still, crime frightens us. We are bombarded by local news shows that begin their coverage every day with blood on the pavement. Motivated by fear, some of us urge our representatives to be "tough on crime," which is often a code phrase for capital punishment.

And so the debate goes on. The time has come for Christians to lower the volume of the shouting voices and, in a spirit of Christian love and humility, listen carefully to each other. Perhaps the key question in this debate is: what would God have us do? Are we to be instruments of His grace or instruments of His justice? Or both?

Notes:
1. Posted in April 2000 on the official web site of Clark County, Indiana.
2. J. J. Maloney, "The Death Penalty," *Crime Magazine*, February 9, 1999, n.p.

Background Scripture: Exodus 21:23-25; John 8:1-11

About the Author: Rev. Gene Van Note is the former executive editor of Sunday School curriculum for the Church of the Nazarene. He is retired and lives in Overland Park, Kansas.

At Issue: When does life end? Under what circumstances can life be prolonged or terminated?

Common Ground: We believe that all human life is sacred. One's relationship to Christ at the time of death determines a person's eternal future.

CHAPTER 12

Euthanasia and Assisted Suicide

by Al Truesdale

Rudy Thompson, a 50-year-old Oregon man, is in the advanced state of Amytrophic Lateral Sclerosis (ALS), a fatal neurological disorder characterized by progressive degeneration of motor cells in the spinal cord and brain. Though Rudy's mind is not impaired, paralysis has slowly spread so that he must now be placed on permanent ventilatory support. His life is confined to his hospital bed.

Rudy has been a Christian for only 5 years. His 70-year-old mother and members of his Sunday School class take care of him. Based on the *Oregon Death with Dignity Act* (1998), Rudy is considering requesting a lethal dose of medicine to end his life. If Rudy proceeds, a physician will prescribe a sufficient supply of barbiturates. Rudy will mix the barbiturates into a chocolate drink, swallow the mixture, and die.

In this chapter we will discuss reasons that attempt to offer a Christian justification for physician-assisted suicide and reasons that supposedly offer convincing Christian reasons to reject physician-assisted suicide. Before presenting both positions, let's define some terms and identify common ground the two sides share.

Definitions

Rudy is considering physician-assisted suicide, a form of euthanasia. The word *euthanasia* comes from two Greek words meaning "good" and "death," hence "a good or easy death." Euthanasia means "mercifully" ending the life of a person whose suffering can only end in death. We usually make a difference between *voluntary* and *involuntary* euthanasia. In the first instance, the person in question consciously chooses euthanasia. In the second, the decision is made for the person by someone else, a family member for example, because the terminally ill person cannot express his or her desire. However, he or she must have given an advance directive prior to becoming incapacitated.

Currently, physician-assisted suicide is the only legal form of euthanasia in the United States. The same is true for Australia and the Netherlands. However, in recent years, books and manuals that tell how to enact euthanasia for oneself have become abundant.

Usually we distinguish between *euthanasia* and *allowing to die*. Euthanasia involves actively terminating a person's death process. Allowing to die means either removing or not engaging artificial life-support systems so that the death process can proceed. On June 25, 1990, in a 5-to-4 decision, the U.S. Supreme Court ruled that American citizens have a right to die. Speaking for the majority, Justice William H. Rehnquist explained that the right to die derives, not from any implicit constitutional guarantee, but from the 14th Amendment's due-process clause. A competent person has a constitutionally protected interest in refusing unwanted medical treatment. A major qualification in the court ruling is that, if during a crisis a person is unable to request that he be allowed to die (e.g., if the person is in a permanent vegetative state), then he or she must have created an "advance directive" while he or she was still competent and coherent.

Most ethicists make a *moral* distinction between *euthanasia* and *allowing to die*. However, there is certainly room for debate about this. Some say that reasons used to support *allowing to die* can also be used to support *euthanasia*.

Common Ground

Regardless of how we might counsel Rudy, there are convictions about which most Christians agree.

First, Christians believe that God is the Creator of human life. Consequently, Christians reject the notion that decisions about either beginning or ending human life can occur simply on the basis of convenience, technology, money, or social status.

Second, Christians believe in "the bestowed value" of human life. Because God is life's Author, we believe that He establishes its value. This is true of all persons, regardless of religion or social standing. Christians reject the notion that persons gain or lose value because of how "useful" or "productive" they are. We don't value human life on the basis of what people can contribute to society. People are not like tools that lose their value when they wear out.

The "bestowed value of life" contrasts with "intrinsic value." If something has intrinsic value, then its significance is established internally. It doesn't need to be valued by someone or for some purpose. By contrast, we Christians believe that human life does have a reference. It has a divinely "bestowed" and hence "inviolable" value. Hence, no one can seize human life and dispose of it as though its significance were under his or her control.

Third, Christians maintain that we are stewards of God's gifts. Stewards manage, they do not own, what another has entrusted to them. Additionally, when stewards return to the Owner what God has entrusted to them, through the quality of their care they should have enriched God's gifts. This is imminently true of human life.

Fourth, Christians believe that personhood gains its ultimate security in God's steadfast love. Unlike those who think that meaning and security come from material well-being, Christians believe that nothing—neither suffering nor death (Romans 8:31-39)—can separate them from the love God displayed toward them in Christ Jesus. Through the centuries, Christian martyrs have demonstrated that Christians don't *have* to live. For Christians, death has lost its sting. Death's claim to have the final word has been silenced.

Fifth, as beneficial as technology is, Christians recognize that failure to place technology under moral and rational restraints is a fatal error. If technology breaks free of religious convictions and moral governance, it will almost certainly destroy the goals it sought to achieve. In the modern era we have often observed a "technological body" bouncing around detached from a "moral head." Christians are not ignorant of technology's benefits. Yet, they also know that in the hands of morally superficial persons, it can be used for barbaric ends.

Finally, Christians are called to worship God alone and to love their neighbor as themselves. The story of the Creator-Redeemer God who sojourns with His people clearly reveals the subtlety of idolatry. All too easily, people—even the people of God—can yield to the temptation to take pieces of the creation and turn them into objects of worship. Our first parents did it by turning away from God and to the tree of knowledge.

At one time or another humankind has labored to convert almost all the parts of creation—including themselves—into "gods." This is no less true of today's sophisticated technology. The objects may change from era to era, but the pattern remains the same. By contrast, Christians believe that we are supposed to worship God alone and to help all creation sing His praise.

When God alone is worshiped instead of our selves or technology, then our neighbor can gain his or her proper place in the creation and in the community. Christians can love and value our neighbor, even as God does. Consequently, in times of crises Christians have no reason to panic by drawing greedily upon the community's human and technical resources. This doesn't block Christians from seeking timely medical assistance. Yet when Christians face death because of age, disease, or illness, they ought not act as idolaters who worship physical existence and who go to every extreme to keep it. Worship of God alone and love for our neighbor should be exhibited in the way Christians *die*. For Christians, that is a "good death."

Issues

Christians can agree on the principles stated so far and still draw significantly different conclusions regarding euthanasia and physician-assisted suicide. Let us first examine premises that claim to support euthanasia as a defensible Christian option.

First, since human life is not an end in itself and should not be clung to as pagans might, Christians can—under some circumstances—actively terminate life and return it to the God who gave it. Mere biological existence, Christians believe, doesn't anchor life's meaning. God alone does that. So to insist that when death is imminent and torturous, we must take from life its last drop of biological existence demonstrates greed and a failure of faith, not faith and worship.

We should explain to Rudy that his security and meaning rest in the Redeemer God, not in a disappearing store of physical existence. Unless someone can show how Rudy's continued torturous physical existence somehow serves an overwhelmingly redemptive purpose, he should be free actively to place his tortured body in God's keeping and elect physician-assisted suicide. Rudy should do so with confidence in God and in hope of the resurrection (1 Corinthians 15:42-58).

Second, let's not make the mistake of worshiping technology in the name of God. Medical technology can sustain Rudy's life for a while, but it can neither reverse ALS nor avert the suffering it causes. Technology must not have the last word. Rudy need not appropriate what technology offers just because of its availability. Technology must not rule. Rudy must be free to declare his dependence on God and elect physician-assisted suicide. By doing so, by rejecting technical heroics, Rudy will show his Christian *respect* for human life, not a *disrespect* as opponents of euthanasia charge.

Third, Christian opponents of euthanasia charge that it is a selfish act because it isolates one from one's family and from Christian support. Quite the opposite is true. Counseling Rudy to forego physician-assisted suicide and to hang onto life until the bitter end only encourages him to act selfishly. Rudy's death is inevitable, only the end of the process is uncertain. In the meantime Rudy will draw unnecessarily upon human and monetary resources that could better be used elsewhere. Why urge him pointlessly to tax public resources to no good end? Doing so only encourages him to violate our Lord's command to love one's neighbor as one's self. In a world where so many people could really benefit from medical resources, let Rudy's election of physician-assisted suicide show how *selflessly* Christians can act. Let him show how much he values the whole human community.

Fourth, while Rudy has already suffered much from ALS, he will likely suffer much more. In some instances, when death is inevitable and the death process is torturous, it is morally permissible and even preferable to intervene directly and mercifully by actively hastening death. Euthanasia releases one from pointless suffering. "Blessed are the merciful," Jesus said (Matthew 5:7). By defensible Christian standards, physician-assisted suicide would extend mercy to Rudy.

Someone will respond, "As Rudy exercises trust during his suffering, he will glorify God. Physician-assisted suicide would keep Rudy from being a blessing to all who look on." To such a response there are three follow-up questions:

1. Just how much suffering is necessary to inspire others?
2. Isn't it rather selfish, if not sadistic, to ask that another suffer so that we might be inspired?
3. Would the questioner himself or herself be willing to refuse a liver transplant, for example, so that his or her suffering might instruct and inspire others?

Fifth, if, as we have said, human life is valuable because it is God's gift and not because of how "productive" it is, then let Rudy elect euthanasia and thereby affirm his faith in God. Let him not hold on to pointless physical existence as though it were *an end in itself.* Let him teach all of us how to avoid treating human life as an idol. As Rudy—a faithful steward—returns to God his 50-year-old tortured body he will teach all of us how to worship God alone!

The Other Side

Let us now examine the major reasons why Christians should reject euthanasia.

First, as Christians we should take counsel from the Bible and from the wisdom of Church history. Consistently, the Early Church fathers strongly opposed euthanasia. Augustine, for example, said:

> It is significant that in Holy Scriptures no passage can be found enjoining or permitting suicide either in order to hasten our entry into immortality or to avoid temporal evils. God's command, "Thou shall not kill," is to be taken as forbidding self-destruction.

Augustine used Romans 8:24-25 to support prohibition against suicide and euthanasia.[1]

The Early Church's prohibition against euthanasia has been upheld by Martin Luther, John Calvin, John Wesley, the Roman Catholics (*Declaration on Euthanasia*, May 5, 1980), the Greek Orthodox Church, the Russian Orthodox Church, the Lutheran Church (Missouri Synod), the Mennonite Church, and the National Association of Evangelicals.

Second, if God is the Author of human life, and if we are God's stewards, then obviously He alone is sovereign over life. To life's very end, Christian stewards must treat life as a gracious and sacred gift, a trust for which we are responsible. Consequently, no Christian can ever set the time for life's termination. Euthanasia violates this principle, for it aggressively seizes control over what one does not own. It breaks God's trust and effectively tosses the gift of life into God's face.

The secular individualism that propels the euthanasia movement treats life as belonging to the person in question. For the secularist, the answer to the question "What should I do?" is preceded by "Whose am I?" And the secularist answers, "I am mine." But when a Christian asks, "Whose am I?" he or she answers, "I am the Lord's." A Christian then asks, "What should I be?" and answers, "A witness in the Church and the world that I belong to Christ, not to myself." Christians must reject euthanasia because the Heavenly Father, not the "god" of secular individualism, shapes their character. Christians believe in God's sovereignty, not in self-sovereignty.

One more part of this first objection is that euthanasia will cheapen life's value in society at large. It conveys the message that human life is just one more disposable thing among others. Damaged? Worn out? Just get rid of it. Euthanasia erodes the fragile yet fundamental respect for human life that makes civilization possible. No Christian can responsibly contribute to this erosion.

Third, while many times suffering serves no good purpose at all (e.g., the rape of a child), there are times when through suffering we can express our rest in God's love that transcends physical pain. The way one bears physical suffering can teach others the power of God's grace, the meaning of faith, and patience. Clearly, the act of euthanasia abruptly terminates all opportunity to learn the power of God's sustaining presence. Euthanasia eliminates the possibility of turning suffering into something redemptive. What if on the Cross Jesus had elected euthanasia?

Euthanasia contributes to our society's fixation on the absence of suffering as life's highest goal. The world's preoccupation with pleasure announces that suffering and meaning are incompatible. Meaning decreases as suffering increases. This materialistic theme is fundamentally at odds with the gospel of our suffering Lord. Physician-assisted suicide feeds the lie.

Fourth, euthanasia, including physician-assisted suicide, is a high act of *selfishness*. It would intentionally cut a person off from Christian fellowship. It would deprive the Christian community of an opportunity to *be* the Church for a sister or brother at life's most difficult stage. Euthanasia denies to one's Christian sisters and brothers any opportunity to minister from Christ's resources. Doubtlessly, Christians can't elect isolation and still act according to Christian virtues. As Christians, the shape of our character has already been determined. We are not free to act in any way we might want. Physician-assisted suicide ignores this.

Fifth, euthanasia steps over a line that should never be crossed. It is perhaps the ultimate expression of human arrogance. It ignores the reality of original sin and humankind's propensity to claim for human wisdom far more than is warranted. Not only Christians, but many others also have recognized the destructive results of human arrogance. Ignoring humankind's fallen state will lead to taking steps that end in destruction. There simply are lines that humans should not cross. Euthanasia is one of them.

In spite of claims to the contrary, euthanasia takes us down a path that leads to a spreading devaluation of human life. Not accidentally, some of the most visible and forceful opponents of euthanasia and physician-assisted suicide are severely disabled people. *The Christian Century* forcefully states the matter:

> What many disabled people can see quite clearly . . . is that the legalization of assisted suicide puts us on a very slippery slope. Once society accepts certain people's "right" to be killed, those who are in similar situations [those who live with severe suffering and infirmities] will have to confront an implicit, perhaps explicit, question: Aren't you better off dead too? [They] will need to justify their continued existence to family, friends, doctors and medical insurers.[2]

Finally, attempting to justify euthanasia because it mercifully relieves suffering as nothing else can ignores the medical community's increasing ability to "manage" pain. Leaders of the hospice movement for example have made major strides in pain management. Currently, the pain of many terminally ill patients is so poorly managed that it often makes euthanasia seem to be the only alternative to pointless suffering. Many patients spend their last days in needless agony, rather than in peace and comfort.

Conclusion

Obviously we have not constructed a united response to Rudy. Hopefully we have gained a stronger appreciation for the topic's complexity. As we progress through this century, numerous technological, social, moral, and religious factors will intensify the importance of Christians carefully examining convictions that apply to end of life issues.

Notes:
1. Walsh, Zema, and Monahan, trans., *Saint Augustine, The City of God* (Garden City, N.Y.: Image Books, 1958), 1:20.

2. "On the Slippery Slope," *The Christian Century,* May 5, 1999, 491.

Background Scripture: Matthew 5:7; Romans 8:24-25, 31-39; 1 Corinthians 15:42-58

About the Author: Dr. Truesdale is professor of Philosophy of Religion and Christian Ethics at Nazarene Theological Seminary, Kansas City.

_____

At Issue: How should Christians respond to war? Should they support it or oppose it?

Common Ground: War is horrible. War results because evil has to be confronted and resisted.

_____

CHAPTER 13

War

by Al Truesdale

In the spring of 1999 Captain John McCord,[1] piloting a Royal Air Force Harrier GR7, made repeated bombing runs over Yugoslavia. He was part of the NATO effort to stop Slobodan Milosovic's program of "ethnic cleansing" in Kosovo.

Captain McCord is a Christian. Some members of his church have sharply criticized his participation in the war. They want him to explain how a Christian can justify dropping bombs that cause death and destruction. A Christian, they insist, should not participate in war. However, other members in the congregation think that as a Christian and as a citizen John McCord has excellent justification for his actions.

The disagreement continues a long-standing debate among Christians: Does being a disciple of Christ prohibit participation in war? After centuries of discussion, Christians have not arrived at a uniform answer. Neither will we. Still, we can identify the ground both sides share, and we can briefly discuss the main reasons each side gives to support its position.

One side is the *pacifist* position. There are numerous forms of Christian pacifism, and there are significant disagreements among pacifists. One well-known author discusses 17 *types* of pacifism.[2] Some pacifists make exceptions that would permit Christian participation in war. Others make no exceptions.

Those on the other side of the debate maintain that

under certain circumstances war and Christian participation in it are justifiable. It may even be required.

Before we examine the two positions, let's discuss the common ground. We should be aware that some of the points of agreement can be used to support either side.

Common Ground

First, Christians agree that love for God and one's neighbor is at the center of the Christian faith. No one who lusts for war as the way to settle international conflicts can legitimately claim to be Christ's follower. Christians must love peace and must try to be peacemakers, if they intend to follow Christ. Diplomacy, not armed conflict, should be the first choice for settling disputes between nations.

Second, Christians agree regarding the sanctity of human life, both individually and communally. They believe that all people have been created in God's image and that they should be treated with respect. Hence, Christians maintain that they have a responsibility for their neighbor's well-being as well as for their own. So anyone who carelessly disregards the value that God places on human life cannot legitimately claim Jesus Christ as Lord.

Third, Christians want to see justice prevail among persons and nations. By justice they mean that all persons should be able to live under conditions that fulfill their potential for individual and communal life. There are fundamental human rights that persons should be free to exercise. Governments exist to secure these rights by promoting justice and social tranquillity, but Christians don't agree on how justice and tranquillity should be achieved. If necessary, should the state use force to correct injustices? If force is sometimes permissible, should it be used only against internal enemies of justice? Or can force be rightly used when the enemy is another nation? Christians have no single answer to these questions.

Fourth, most Christians agree that civil government plays at least some legitimate role in God's scheme of things. One of its chief responsibilities is to protect citizens against abuse by those who want to exploit them, but there is no agreement about the Christian's proper relationship to the state. Nor is there agreement about the appropriate limits of the state's authority over Christians.

Fifth, all Christians adhere to the sixth commandment, "Thou shalt not kill" (Exodus 20:13, KJV). Most pacifists believe that the word "kill" refers not only to murder but also to the killing that occurs in war. Those on the other side, who think that Christians can participate in war, also embrace the sixth commandment. However, they believe that the commandment prohibits "murder," but not killing enemy combatants in a time of war. While "murder" serves no redemptive purpose, they say, war can and often does.

Sixth, all Christians believe that the Bible should have the final say regarding war. But here the agreement ends. The Bible seems to provide ample support for both pacifists and supporters of limited war.

Seventh, most Christians agree that humankind is fallen and that our fallen state should be taken seriously when answering questions regarding war. Yet, from this fundamental agreement Christians draw conflicting conclusions.

Finally, both sides appeal to reason and to the lessons of human experience, but they draw different conclusions about what reason and history teach us. Each side can say, "Look carefully at the history of humankind's wars, and you will see that our position is vindicated."

Pacifism's Viewpoint

Let us first hear from the pacifist position. Keep in mind that pacifism is quite diverse and cannot receive full treatment here. We will examine the absolutist form of pacifism, which holds that under no conditions should

Christians support war, either indirectly or as combatants. Initially at least, the pacifist position appears to be conclusive and to make other options seem unfaithful to Jesus' instructions. For this position, the question regarding Christian participation in war boils down to whether or not one wants to be a faithful disciple of Jesus Christ.

First and perhaps most importantly, Jesus' Sermon on the Mount stands as the Rock of Gibraltar in this debate. Here (Matthew 5—7 and Luke 6:17-49) Jesus reveals the radical difference between the old order of vengeance and the new order—the kingdom of God. This is the order of suffering, redemptive love. It is the Kingdom of peace. The goals and ways of the old order are simply not those of the kingdom of God. Those who want to enter the kingdom of God had better look closely at what citizenship requires. Few there are who will place their trust in God rather than in violence. Candidates for the Kingdom must recognize that the old way of resolving conflicts and of halting aggressors has given way to suffering, redemptive love. The kingdom of darkness and the kingdom of God are irreconcilable. So if a person is not yet finished with the old order of vengeance, then he or she should not try to embrace the kingdom of God.

In the new order, God gives the kingdom of heaven to those who are gentle and lowly, to those who are merciful and who work for peace through suffering love. These "blessed" ones can see further than violence can ever see. If there are still doubts about what Jesus thought of violence, listen carefully: "I tell you, Do not resist an evil person. If someone strikes you on the right cheek, turn to him the other also" (Matthew 5:39). "I tell you: Love your enemies and pray for those who persecute you" (5:44).

Search as we might, we find no exceptions to Jesus' instructions. Our options are either to accept Jesus' words and enter the kingdom of God or to reject them and remain in the kingdom of darkness.

Second, the kingdom of God is founded upon the love of God, not upon the violence and foolishness of humans. We know that the God who is love *(agapē)* seeks reconciliation (John 3:16), not cycles of violent alienation. Furthermore, God's love is a suffering love that seeks to reconcile, not to destroy, His enemies. To that end, God willingly takes the sin of the world upon himself. The great Servant Songs of Isaiah and their fulfillment in Jesus affirm this.

Throughout Jesus' earthly ministry, He absorbed the taunts of His enemies without resorting to violence. Ultimately, Jesus exemplified the Sermon on the Mount on the Cross. He died willingly in the service of love, though He could have placed 12 legions[3] of angels in battle formation (see Matthew 26:53).

Christians who think there are times when they can set aside Jesus' teachings and act contrary to the example He established for us should recognize their arrogance and unbelief. Throughout church history, some Christians have been willing to distort Jesus' teachings beyond recognition, but all such efforts finally mock those who follow this course. Faced with the *consequences* of war, they will see that they have betrayed the Prince of Peace.

If someone responds, "But that's not practical in a world like this," then they will have to argue with Jesus on the Cross. Predictably, following Jesus will be countercultural, costly, and difficult. Nevertheless, didn't Jesus tell us that we should not expect to be above Him (Matthew 10:24-26)? Breaking the cycles of violence that enslave the earth and promoting reconciliation among people will indeed be costly. Still, the Church has been commissioned to give witness to an alternative world. If the Church fails in its commission and resorts to the violence of war, then she will have hidden her light under a bushel. Let us not try to baptize the old order in Jesus' name!

Third, pacifism expresses faith in God, not in armed might. War is a failure of faith. In the face of what appear to be urgent and justifiable reasons for war, Christians must "be still, and know that I am God" (Psalm 46:10). They should "wait quietly for the salvation of the LORD" (Lamentations 3:26). Unlike those who can see no further than settling disputes through war, Christians should trust in the sovereign God who rules this world according to His wisdom.

Christians who cobble together ways to get around Jesus' instructions cannot hide the fact that they are faithless servants.

Fourth, contrary to popular opinion, Jesus' followers are actually the farsighted ones. They are not the naive, shortsighted folk their critics describe. In fact, deploying tanks, missiles, and bombs to solve international conflicts is shortsighted and counterproductive. War promises to resolve conflicts, but it doesn't. Resorting to war ignores other and better (even if more difficult) options. It succeeds only in generating hatred and violence that works its way into a nation's soul. In the long run, war erodes both winners and losers. Defeated people believe that they have been victimized, and their desire for revenge grows as selective memory reshapes the past. For generations to come, Serbs and ethnic Albanians in Kosovo will nurse hatred and vengeance toward each other.

Pacifism, by contrast, takes the long view. The best and Christian way to break cycles of violence is to refuse to feed them. Refusing to resort to war keeps the roots of hatred from spreading. Those who listen to Jesus and refuse to resist evil through violence avert multiplying the hatreds that currently plague our world.

Pacifists read history and think that it demonstrates the rightness of pacifism. What has the long history of war gotten us? Peace in the world? Nations and religions that are more tolerant of each other? Has the net effect of war relaxed the burden of war debt placed upon subsequent generations? When a nation spends its human and physical resources to make war, the costs will be charged against its children for generations to come. Violence becomes part of that nation's genetic code and expresses itself in countless ways.

Fifth, Christians owe their allegiance to Christ, not to the state. The state has the power to tax, to declare and make war, and it can imprison those who do not comply. Still, Christians must resist the pressure to place allegiance to the state above allegiance to Christ. Yielding to such pressure is exactly what participation in war is. Engagement in war supports a form of idolatry, the idolatry of nationalism. Even at the cost of their lives, Christians ought to show that God places limits on the state.

If Christians will keep their primary allegiance clear, they will be able to speak as prophets against the deification of the state and the lunacy of war. Think of what would happen if Christians worldwide would say to their governments, "We owe our allegiance to Christ, not to you. We will not be a party to your faithlessness and your love affair with violence." When Christians around the world put being Christians ahead of being Russians, Chinese, Germans, or Americans, then the arrogance that makes war possible will be broken.

The Conflicting View

Christians who believe that pacifists are wrong certainly do not discredit their ideals. They, too, believe that Jesus inaugurated the kingdom of God. They also are aware that once war begins, no one can control its tragedies. They agree that conflicts among nations should be resolved peacefully, if possible. They, too, pray for peace upon the earth. Let us examine some of the major reasons Christians give for justifying participation in war.

First, when pacifists use Jesus' Sermon on the Mount to oppose all war, they make a terrible mistake. The Sermon on the Mount is not a blueprint for organizing secular society. Nor is it a drawing for how Christians should exercise their citizenship in a secular state. Jesus' instructions to His disciples about refusing to resist an evil person and turning the other cheek involve individual responses, not social policy. As individuals, we should not choose violence for responding to offenses against us.

No nation can fulfill its responsibilities to its citizens and at the same time act according to the Sermon on the Mount. Neither can a Christian execute his or her responsibilities as a citizen in that way. The major function of a state is to insure conditions under which persons can peacefully fulfill their familial and public duties. Under state protection, people should be free to pursue a livelihood and provide for their families in an atmosphere free of threat. Any nation that fails to protect its citizens thereby defaults on its inherent, God-given commission. Tragically, sometimes a state must resort to war to fulfill its responsibilities (Romans 13:1-7).

Second, a state's legitimate use of force does not begin with war. It begins with the police who patrol our streets and protect us against society's enemies. It continues with arresting, trying, and incarcerating criminals. Christians who accept police protection either for themselves or for their neighbors have already endorsed a certain form of violence. In some instances, to fulfill its mandate, a state must use force to repel foreign threats to social well-being.

Even if this is true, aren't Christians exceptions to the secular rule? Are they not committed to a higher law, the law of love that prohibits participation in war?

Christians who make this claim do so at the expense of consistent thought. Citizenship is not something one can step into and out of at will. Like all other citizens, Christians too benefit from state services such as fire and police protection. They cannot insist on such services and then conveniently choose another set of rules when the structures upon which society depends come under attack from a foreign foe.

Christians who embrace pacifism do so either hypo-critically or naively. They readily accept the benefits of cit-izenship but are then unwilling to pay the price needed to preserve it. The pacifist can enjoy the luxury of pacifism only because someone else foots the bill. Unless a Chris-tian is willing completely to remove himself or herself and his or her family from state protection and benefits, then let him or her (while recognizing the tragedy of war) aban-don the pacifist illusion.

Third, while pacifists correctly insist that love for God and one's neighbor is the rule of Christian faith, they blindly overlook another central Christian doctrine, the doctrine of original sin. The notion that expressing Chris-tian love towards an aggressor by rejecting all violence will somehow turn him or her away from violence naively ig-nores a perversity that plagues the human race. Not only is evil individually evident in persons, it also appears as an aggressive kingdom. Evil is manifested in individual acts and in demonic structures of destruction. It is the na-ture of evil structures to spread strife and oppression. Some evil structures can be toppled only by superior mili-tary force. Nazism illustrated this well.

No doubt there are times when the power of God's love does subdue the power of evil. It converted the dark heart of former slave trader, John Newton, author of "Amazing Grace." Still, in the face of organized aggression by a military power, the elected officials sworn to protect the state cannot simply wait to see whether love will over-come the aggressor. Any public official and any citizen who would do this could not at the same time properly show love to one's neighbors. Love in the form of fulfilling one's public and private responsibilities will require the state to use all available resources to halt aggression. The Christian ought not evade this responsibility.

Fourth, while it is true that Christ inaugurated the kingdom of God on earth, that Kingdom has not yet been completed. There is often an ugly gap between the *already* and the *not yet*. Until the day when the *not yet* is overcome and the kingdom of God fully comes, all responsible citizens—Christians included—must be prepared to deal realistically with the *not yet*. This is "Christian realism." Until God completes His kingdom on earth, Christians, along with others, must realistically confront kingdoms that have not yet yielded to Christ (1 Corinthians 15:24-25). This is what Captain McCord was doing in the skies over Yugoslavia. The 20th century witnessed unforgettable instances of the *not yet*. Governments given to evil have used military power to tyrannize and enslave others.

By refusing Christian participation in war, pacifists naively act as though the *not yet* has already been overcome. Christians who are unwilling to take their places alongside those who deal realistically with the *not yet* neither appreciate the importance of social stability nor properly understand the kingdom of God.

Notes:
  1. *Captain McCord is a fictional character.
  2. John Howard Yoder, *Nevertheless: Varieties of Religious Pacifism* (Scottdale, Pa.: Herald Press, 1992).
  3. Twelve legions would be somewhere between 36,000 and 72,000 troops.

Background Scripture: Exodus 20:13; Psalm 46:10; Lamentations 3:26; Matthew 5—7; 10:24-26; 26:53; Luke 6:17-49; John 3:16; Romans 13:1-7; 1 Corinthians 15:24-25

About the Author: Dr. Truesdale is professor of Philosophy of Religion and Christian Ethics at Nazarene Theological Seminary, Kansas City.